Phenomenology

SUNY Series in Contemporary Continental Philosophy

Dennis J. Schmidt, Editor

PHENOMENOLOGY

Jean-François Lyotard

Translated by Brian Beakley
Foreword by Gayle L. Ormiston

State University of New York Press

Phenomenology is translated from *La phénoménologie,* tenth edition, by Jean-François Lyotard, © 1986 Presses Universitaires de France.

Published by
State University of New York Press, Albany

For information, address State University of New York
Press, State University Plaza, Albany, N.Y. 12246

Production by Dana Foote
Marketing by Theresa A. Swierzowski

Library of Congress Cataloging-in-Publication Data

Lyotard, Jean-François.
    [Phénoménologie. English]
    Phenomenology / Jean-François Lyotard ; translated by Brian
Beakley ; with a Foreword by Gayle L. Ormiston.
        p.   cm. — (SUNY series in contemporary continental
philosophy)
    Translation of: La phénoménologie.
    Includes bibliographical references and index.
    ISBN 0–7914–0805–1 (alk. paper) . — ISBN 0–7914–0806–X pbk. :
alk. paper)
    1. Phenomenology. I. Title. II. Series.
B829.5.L92   1991
142' .7—dc20
                                                            90–19828
                                                            CIP

10 9 8 7 6 5 4 3 2 1

Contents

Foreword

In the midst...multiplicities...always beginnings: An Introduction to Lyotard's Phenomenological Episodes

Gayle L. Ormiston

> ...I suggest that each thinking consists in a re-
> thinking and that there is nothing the presenta-
> tion of which could be said to be the "premiere."
> Every emergence of something reiterates some-
> thing else, every occurrence is a recurrence, not
> at all in the sense that it could repeat the same
> thing or be the rehearsal or the same play, but in
> the sense of the Freudian notion of the
> *Nachträglich*, the way the first offense touches
> our mind too soon and the second too late, so
> that the first time is like a thought not yet thought
> while the second time is like a not-thought to be
> thought later.
>
> Jean-François Lyotard
> *Peregrinations: Law, Form, Event*[1]

1. Soliciting Philosophy's Histories

According to its dates of publication and its thematic orienta-
tions, Jean-François Lyotard's *Phenomenology* marks a particular episode—initials specific links—in his persistent reflection on
the "philosophical project."[2] More specifically, *Phenomenology*
presents a commentary on the express philosophical projects of

the phenomenological movement. From the diverse perspectives of a work *on* and *of* phenomenology, Lyotard's text profiles the different "accents," as he says, that mark phenomenology. As such, it is emblematic of certain "critical" practices or reflections—"radical" reflections, some might wish to say[3]—associated with particular motifs of phenomenology and carried out on what otherwise might be termed the "mundane" questions and causes or the "routine" commitments and involvements with which philosophy comes to concern itself. In the language of *Phenomenology,* such projects turn on the intentional analysis of the *lifeworld* (*Lebenswelt*), the intricate weaving of the "subjective" (transcendental or otherwise) and the "intersubjective."

To be sure, according to Lyotard "the value of phenomenology, its 'positive side' lies in its effort to recover humanity itself, beneath any objectivist schema, which the human sciences can never recover; and any dialogue with phenomenology clearly must take place on this basis" (136).[4] Thus, Lyotard's *Phenomenology* is always (and already) involved in rethinking the contingencies and facts that comprise the matrix of intersubjectivity, or what in Husserl's texts is a "nexus of supplementation."[5] For Lyotard, phenomenology "reawakens" (to use Merleau-Ponty's phrase) one's sensibilities and sentiments toward the inextricable involvements of consciousness and history. In other words, phenomenology in particular, and philosophy engaged in specific contexts and conditions in general, is a *recollection*—an *anámnesis*—of the subtleties involved in an ongoing genesis of contingency and fact, passive/active synthesis and consciousness.[6] And to be sure, anámnesis is itself a phenomenological tool.[7] As such, *Phenomenology* elaborates upon, by way of a series of its own imaginative variations, what Lyotard identifies as "the first great Husserlian process," the recognition that to think the contingency of a "fact" is "to think that *it belongs to the essence of the fact that it could be otherwise*" (41, emphasis added). Conceived in these terms, *Phenomenology* is an initial episode in a series of experiments *soliciting* philosophy, simultaneously seeking to realize philosophy and demanding that philosophy see itself "eliminated as a separated existence" (136).[8] Thus, Lyotard's phenomenological analysis demonstrates the extent to which phenomenology always and already has been involved in seeking radically new beginnings. That is to say, Lyotard's *Phenomenology* demonstrates the extent to which phenomenology always and already has been involved in sounding "the knell of the age of the Professor"![9]

Indeed, "after having rendered unto Husserl that which is Husserl's," after having acknowledged and accounted for the beginnings and the infinite tasks already having been begun by this Professor (the achievements of the emphasis on "realism" of essences articulated in the *Logical Investigations,* the focus on the transcendental radicality of "subjectivity" presented in the *Cartesian Meditations,* and the proclamations regarding "inter-subjectivity" and the "lifeworld" stated in *The Crisis*), Lyotard pursues the ambiguities and complexities of phenomenology's histories. Like any other philosophical stance presented as a "critique of Philosophy," like other attempts to supply a new "foundation" for the natural and human sciences, which are ruled by a certain naivety regarding the "origins" of their knowledge and point of departure, and like other moments in the so-called critique of metaphysics, phenomenology is "rooted in a heritage" (32). "Thus history envelops phenomenology": a disconcerting truth, a bane which marks Husserl's work from the beginning to the end. So, despite a certain "ahistorical pretention in phenomenology," phenomenology must be approached through its history. In doing so, Lyotard claims to "leave it [phenomenology] in its debates with history" (ibid).

> ...we can grasp history neither through objectivism nor subjectivism, and even less through a problematic union of the two, but only through a deepening of both which leads us to the very existence of historical subjects in their "world," on the basis of which objectivism and subjectivism appear as two equally inadequate options through which these subjects can understand themselves in history.... Because history [the history of human subjects as well as the history of phenomenology] is never completed—that is, because it is human—it is not a specifiable object; but precisely because it is human, history is not meaningless. Thus we find a new justification for the Husserlian motif of a philosophy which is never finished with the question of a "radical beginning" (131–32).

2. Anámnesis and the Forgotten Initial

Furthermore, Lyotard's *Phenomenology* signifies an initial episode that has been forgotten or, at least, an episode that has been neglected in the recent upsurge of interest in his work. It recalls an episode that has been overshadowed, perhaps, due to the constant transformation and displacement—the constant reinscription—of many of its themes and desires in subsequent texts that seem more in synch with the poststructural-decon-struction signatures and postmodern conditions of the times.[10] In many ways, it recalls an initial episode, initial thoughts that perhaps came too soon or too late. Perhaps too soon or too late following the publication of Merleau-Ponty's *Phenomenology of Perception* and *Humanism and Terror?* Perhaps too soon or too late, before or after recognizing a differend with specific elements of Marxism and French Socialism in the general press to create certain links between phenomenology and Marxism?

Perhaps it recalls an episode that appears too soon or too late today as well? Perhaps Lyotard's *Phenomenology* attempts to present today—just as it had in 1954—something that cannot be thought at a specific moment, by Husserl, Heidegger, Merleau-Ponty, Lyotard, or by others—links that remain unpresentable? A crisis of sorts, perhaps a crisis of "having begun," a crisis of being enveloped by history and, at the same time, desiring completion or certainty?

Perhaps Lyotard's *Phenomenology* presents today—just as it had in 1954—a new tempo or various tempos, ones that threaten from inside the time or times in which they appear—tempos that recall Hamlet's announcement that "the time is out of joint."[11] Perhaps *Phenomenology* presents an episode or initially forgotten episodes that alter the reading of the present once reinserted in a sequence of current episodes and intervals.

To be sure, according to many contemporary "observers," phenomenology is a little outdated, passé, a little bit of history. And if it is history, then how can it be current? Has phenomenology not been negated and superseded where its insights and truths, as well as its follies and untruths, have been synthesized into "our" contemporary consciousness? How can it work effectively within the breadth and depth of "our" new sophistication?

Under this kind of interrogation, *phenomenology* does not seem to fit with the currents of contemporary philosophy in general, nor with the emergent issues that face philosophers today.

In the midst of a contemporary philosophical scene, among certain practices and institutions in the United States, Great Britain, France, Germany, and Italy, where modes of inquiry and "rational" discourse are apparently preoccupied by the apocalyptic and enlightened tones regarding "our" postmodern condition, the "truths" of poststructuralism, deconstruction, and the general critique of the metaphysics of grand narratives, the English translation and publication of a text on phenomenology, particularly Lyotard's *Phenomenology,* and one so simply titled, *may* appear strikingly out of fashion. But perhaps the apparent simplicity of Lyotard's *Phenomenology,* its orderliness and organization, does not fully divulge its subtleties and multiplicities—the tensions and contradictions revealed in its descriptions and analyses? Perhaps its striking economy betrays its episodic structure, that is, the differends that provoke and orient its reflections?

In the midst of certain prevailing modes of thought, where talk about overcoming metaphysics, the end of systematic philosophy, and the need to *replace* the culture of "first philosophy" and the methods based upon "first principles" with the poetics of play is persistent and commonplace, "phenomenology"—as a particular philosophical tradition, school of thought, or philosophical "method"—*may* appear out of synch, something like a conceptual anachronism. Moreover, in the midst of the imbroglio of concerns over various philosophical and literary "affairs" or "involvements" in politics, the links between philosophy and action—what might be called the connections (inherent or foreign) between the "thought" and the "life" of a "thinker"—phenomenology *may* strike many as an intriguing but archaic mode of thought, another once highly valued but outdated trinket that amused and engaged philosophy once, but failed. Today, on these grounds, it would scarcely be considered a gem or an enticing jewel.

Failed? Has it failed? And if so, why? How? By what standards, according to whose criteria has phenomenology failed? Because of the requirements it established but was unable to meet? Because of requirements for the primordial status of intentionality, that consciousness is always the consciousness *of* something? Because of a demand for "foundations," a *Mathesis Universalis?* "Essences"? "Egos"—transcendental and otherwise? "Ideational variation?" Because of a demand for the *epoché,* for "bracketing" or putting in "parentheses" the natural attitude? Has phenomenology failed because of, perhaps in spite of, a *desire* for the "things themselves"? Has phenomenology failed because it began as a critique of metaphysics and turned out to be just a little too much "pure" metaphysics for "our" blood today?

But is not perceiving, conceiving, and interpreting phenomenology only in these terms to idealize, to fictionalize phenomenology? Does it not amount to arresting phenomenology, categorizing it, so it fits neatly into certain contemporary idioms? So that it—phenomenology itself—appears solely in a predetermined manner, prepredicated as it were, without any notice of its continual transformation in subsequent uses and practices? Does it not amount to fixing the "essence" of phenomenology so that it can be comprehended, digested, catalogued, and made academic, that is to say, betrayed, turned into a separated existence? Does is not amount to a purposeful neglect of the differences and differends generated by those persons who put phenomenology into practice? If so, does this idealization of phenomenology not also indicate a kind of *rigor* of conception—a stiffness, an inflexibility—presumed for philosophy in general? After all, are there not other terms and phrases, other ways of linking up with phenomenology (philosophy)?

In attempting to retrace the many paths and motifs of phenomenology—as Lyotard demonstrates, paths that lead in and out of phenomenology, as well as paths that traverse the diverse conceptions of the phenomenological project—Lyotard's discourse is always reflective, philosophic, *meta,* taking as its object certain phrases in dispute, certain links made to constitute the phenomenological project. He elicits a recollection of what is already and always presupposed and buried in contemporary practices of philosophy, the practices of connecting phrases in seemingly already specified ways. In effect, Lyotard's *Phenomenology* solicits an attempt to recall the sites of some "initial forgetting." So, to ask a question Lyotard himself poses in the text: "Why 'phenomenology'?"

The term signifies a study of "phenomena," that is to say, of *that* which appears to consciousness, *that* which is "given" (32).... In the place of the traditional consciousness which "digests," or at least ingests, the external world (as in Condillac, for example), phenomenology reveals a consciousness which "bursts outward" (Sartre)—*a consciousness, in sum, which is nothing if not a relation to the world* (33–34, emphasis added).

It is in this respect that Lyotard's *Phenomenology* is reminiscent of certain styles of analysis, certain *façons de parler* found his later works, such as *The Postmodern Condition* (1979), *The Differend* (1983), and *Peregrinations* (1988). However, this is also to say there is a redoubling of reminiscence: the latter works recall or reawaken the analysis of *Phenomenology* as well, even works like *Discours, Figure* (1971), *Economie libidinal* (1974), or *Rudiments païens: Genre dissertatif* (1977). Both as the title of the work *and* as the name of a particular philosophical method, *Phenomenology* identifies, signifies, or, beyond accounting for a particular episode, marks the recognition of a "nexus of horizons"—ambiguities and differends. Lyotard states that his exposé will not attempt to "erase" the ambiguities, the betrayal, the dialectical movement of phenomenology, nor will it blur the differences in "accents" "inscribed...in the very history of the phenomenological school" (33). Instead, his exposition will examine the differences, the dissent, the episodes, or, as he might say in the idiom of *The Differend,* the "cases of differend and to find the rules for the heterogeneous genres of discourses that bring about these cases."[12]

Phenomenology is a "philosophical" discourse; it is not an "academic," "textbook" account of phenomenology as a philosophical method or school.[13] It is a philosophical discourse, as opposed to a "theoretical" treatise, in that it attempts to discover or to recall the rules, prejudices, and ambiguities that structure or constitute a particular moment—the concentration of particular forms—in phenomenological analysis. It is in this respect that Lyotard supplies a *phenomenology of phenomenology.* As such, Lyotard does not assume any truth or knowledge that, in principle, can be associated with phenomenology. Its truths can be known only through its experiences.

According to its own desires, according to its historical presence and conditions, according to its own "essential" variations, the truths and meanings of phenomenology lie before it, never yet fully articulated, only profiled. And yet, Lyotard writes, "We will have to fix its historical significance even though this is not ascribable once and for all..." (34) But why can the significance of phenomenology not be assigned "once and for all"? Because "to fix" its historical significance, to fix any meaning whatsoever, is itself to constitute an "idealizing fiction," a fiction that simplifies and brings together the continuous and successive "flux" and pluralities of perspective and profile at work in describing any phenomenon, event, or object as it appears. And given successive and unending profiling of imaginative variation, the fictionalized ideal is transformed as well. As Lyotard notes later in the text:

> In the course of perception the successive profiles are altered, and a new perspective of the object can come to correct an earlier one; there is no contradiction here— since the flux of all these perspectives merges into the unity of one perception—but only the object emerging throughout these alterations without end (48).

Moreover, the historical significance of phenomenology cannot be assigned in any definite or final form because "there are presently *many* phenomenologists," and "its [phenomenology's] meaning is still 'in process,' unfinished precisely because it is historical. There are, in effect, different 'accents' from Heidegger to Fink, from Merleau-Ponty to Ricoeur, from Pos or Thevanez to Levinas, which justify the prudence with which we will begin" (34). It is for these reasons, once again invoking the language of *The Differend,* that Lyotard's phenomenology "denies itself the possibility of settling, on the basis of its own rules, the differends it examines..."[14]

3. From the Postmodern to the Phenomenological

Phenomenology, then, presents an initial episode, perhaps forgotten. But it is an episode in which Lyotard states very clearly that there is not, nor can there be, a "common measure" or "procedure" that mediates the differend of idioms: there can be no "common code" that can be deciphered or employed to decipher the multiplicity of accents that mark phenomenological undertakings. There can be no "third language" that has been or will have been "instituted to establish" a "fixed" reality underlying all determinations.[15] For to presume such a mechanism or to supply such a discourse would require taking up a position "outside" the fray, and in this case, as in all cases with Lyotard, even the *meta-position* is very much involved in the disputes and conflicts it identifies, explores, explicates, and would attempt to mediate. The phenomenological reduction—that is, the suspension of prejudices or conflicts that arise because of these presuppositions—is never complete.

With every thinking there is a rethinking, a re-collecting that modifies the parameters of the debate, transforms the differend by the very fact that the issues or the contentious points have been (and will have been) recontextualized, recited, and recalled for a particular purpose. Every reconstruction, every anámnesis involves a "rupture in the order of things."[16] So to outline a "common phenomenological 'style'" (34) is not to adumbrate a common code. Even though he will not be able to "localize the finer or coarser divergences which separate these philosophers" (ibid), the analysis of "phenomenology" will *supplement* Lyotard's attempt to rethink—incessantly profiling, redescribing, and rephrasing—the nature and the ambiguity of the phenomenological event—that particular episode in which his analysis is always and already caught or having begun.

One of the most striking features of Jean-François Lyotard's *thought* is its episodic character, that is to say, its diversity, its plurality, its "schizzes," and the recognition of its own transient character.[17] Indeed, Lyotard is very aware of the fragmentary and transitory constitution of thought. In *Peregrinations,* he says, "When I seem totally committed to a line of force...I am actually not, for I am also looking to the side at the other lines and inhabited by a kind of jealousy mixed with eagerness."[18] Moreover, in a very "phenomenological" way, he notes that when he says, for example, "Being is definitely elusive," or when he reiterates Aristotle's point that "Being does not give itself as such, but *only through different aspects,"* he is using a metaphor to describe "nothing but the condition of thinking insofar as it takes into account the principle of relativity it is affected by."[19] It is a relativity which each thinking, writing, and action must take into account in order to grasp its own provisional character as it emerges from and reinserts itself into the contingent sources of facts and history. "Meaning cannot in any sense be taken for granted," Lyotard writes in the *Phenomenology,* "and history cannot be read through any single 'factor,' be it political, economic, or racial" (123). Thus, he repeats, as a truth of phenomenology, but not as a mere rehearsal of a "truth," a theme announced first by Merleau-Ponty in the "Preface" to the *Phenomenology of Perception:*

> We find in texts only what we put into them.... We shall find in ourselves, and nowhere else, the unity and true meaning of phenomenology. It is less a question of counting up quotations than of determining and expressing in concrete form this *phenomenology for ourselves* which has given a number of present-day readers the impression, on reading Husserl and Heidegger, not so much of encountering a new philosophy as of recognizing what they had been waiting for. Phenomenology is accessible only through a phenomenological method. Let us, therefore, try systematically to bring together the celebrated phenomenological themes as they have grown spontaneously together in life. Perhaps we shall then understand why phenomenology has for so long remained at an initial stage, as a problem to be solved and a hope to be realized.[20]

Lyotard recapitulates in the following manner:

> It is true that the meaning of this "movement," or "style," can only be fixed if one investigates its interior, taking upon oneself the question it bears; one would say as much of Marxism or Cartesianism. This signifies, in short, that philosophy must not be only grasped as event, and "from the outside," but worked through as thought—that is as problem, genesis, give-and-take

movement of thought. This constitutes the genuine objectivity that Husserl wanted...(31).[21]

So to notice the "episodic" in Lyotard's "thought," that is to say, his philosophical writings, artistic activities, and political engagements, is not, on the one hand, to notice or to invoke the necessity of a "historical development" that can be traced from the "outside." It is not to raise the necessity of an individual odyssey according to which Lyotard can *or* cannot (should *or* should not) be read, as if there were a succession to presuppose and recover. Moreover, it is not to invoke the idea of intellectual or philosophical "progress" that has taken place over a series of periods or temporal moments, represented in various texts. To advance the necessity of factuality, the "fact" of such a development, is tantamount to the view that the most recent episode necessarily supersedes and nullifies each of the antecedent stages. According to such a view, one can separate and isolate early, middle, and late "Lyotard" periods, as so many commentators are wont to do with other figures in contemporary thought, such as Husserl, Wittgenstein, Heidegger, and Dewey. But this amounts to a selective neglect of the contingencies and variations at work that make the fact possible and recognizable as such.

On the other hand, suppressing the contingencies of historical development amounts to a denial of the contextual character of philosophical investigations, a disavowal of what might be termed the "pragmatic necessities," that is, the specific contexts and purposes of any inquiry, along with the conditions to which an inquiry responds and the desires that provoke it. It would amount to a neglect, an *amnesia* certainly not an anámnesis, of those particular pragmatic necessities and formations that result in the generation of differences, the multiplicity of differences in perspectives and thematics, from one moment to the next.

Nor is "episodic" used here to represent Lyotard's peregrinations as mere wanderings—aimless, digressive, and meandering excursions. From the very early review of Karl Jaspers's *Die Schuldfrage: Ein Beitrag sur deutschen Frage* (1948); through the work on *Socialisme ou Barbarie* (1954–64) and *Pouvoir Ouvrier* (1964–68); through the "philosophical" interrogations of certain boundaries that separate academic disciplines (or intellectual real estate) undertaken in *Discours, Figure, Economie libidinal,* or *Just Gaming* and *The Postmodern Condition* (both from 1979), and the art exhibit, *Les Immateriaux,* staged at the Centre Georges Pompidou (1985); up through more recent work on *The Differend* and *Heidegger and the Jews* (1987), Lyotard acknowledges and accommodates—*pursues*—the opening of pathways relative to specific desires and interests, contingencies and facts—relative to specific practical involvements.

To mark out or to focus on the episodic character of Lyotard's thought is to see each moment of its history, each period in its development or succession, or each text as an act of moving into (not merely towards) an entrance, marking a point of entry, or indicating an intersection or a threshold between one *hodos* (way) and others. The episodic can be seen as a sign of where shifts in thought occur, where translation is required, and where reiteration and supplementation are presupposed. Why? Because of the flux of multiplicities: "everything changes," as Deleuze notes in his remarks on Kant; and relativity affects the conception of change.[22] And the success or succession of change requires bridging gaps—supplying that which is absent—by way of reiteration and supplementation, never by presenting the absent itself through the sensible presence of a fiction (or representation) but through the constitution, that is, the presentation of what will have been.

But the episodic is more than an alert, a signal, or a way of recognizing that one is always "in the midst" or always "having begun." It simultaneously flags a point of departure, a *beginning,* a point from which connections or linkings are to be made, out of necessity constituted. It indicates, advances, and moreover recapitulates a leitmotif of phenomenology: one is *always and already* beginning; beginning is the constant state for the philosopher. For as Lyotard notes in *The Postmodern Condition,* a philosopher is "not an expert." "The latter knows what he knows and what he does not know: the former does not. One concludes, the other questions—two very different language games."[23] And in the context of Lyotard's phenomenological ruminations, to question is to presuppose an open-ended field of variation or phrasing.

The inconclusive character of the episode, the perpetual state of beginning it elicits, or the "unfinished nature of phenomenology" is not "a sign of failure," as Merleau-Ponty notes.[24] Lyotard agrees: in fact one can imagine *Phenomenology* as a "sign of history," an indication "that something which should be able to be put into phrases cannot be phrased in the accepted idioms."[25] And as a sign of history, Lyotard's phenomenological phrasings always mark one more (but only one?) "border zone," perhaps a forgotten initial episode or initial intersection, "where genres of discourse," the different "accents" of phenomenology, "enter into conflict over the mode of linking."[26] But these phrasings of phenomenology also present that border zone, that idealizing fiction "in which the differend between genres of discourse," the differend between the naive and the philosophic, the differend between the pagan and the philosopher, "is suspended."[27] As a sign of history, *Phenomenology* reawakens and disturbs the sedimentation of so much history. Is Lyotard's differend with phenomenology, his sign of history, not yet another episode in or yet another variation on a theme or aspect buried in Merleau-Ponty's *Phenomenology of Perception?*

> The phenomenological world is not pure being, but the sense which is revealed where the paths of my various experiences intersect, and also where my own and other people's intersect and engage each other like gears.[28]

Is Lyotard's differend not yet another recapitulation of Merleau-Ponty's *chiasm,* as it is articulated in *The Visible and the Invisible?*

> *And what we have to understand is that there is no dialectical reversal from one of these views to the other; we do not have to reassemble them into a synthesis: they are two aspects of the reversibility which is the ultimate truth* (emphasis added).[29]

Is it not yet another episode in realizing "the most important lesson which the reduction teaches us is the impossibility of a complete reduction"?[30]

As the sign of history, the episodic then always bears its multiplicities and variations as the possibilities of its existence. The episodic always signifies the necessity of linking, making connections, and noticing it could be otherwise. In this respect, the episodic always marks a "middle" in Lyotard's idiom; and Lyotard (or by analogy, anyone) is always caught in the middle, in the midst of diverging pathways, in between specific ways of speaking, in between specific modes of thought, in "the middle of things," in "the middle of time."[31]

Here the notion of *middle* can be likened to the kind of inter-val—perhaps an intermezzo—one finds in the performance and study of certain musical forms, where the episode is taken as any incidental passage between recapitulations of a theme or an arrangement of themes. One always begins in the middle, amidst the flux and relativity—the contingency—of possible, alternative paths, phrasings, and framings. The interval alludes to the emer-gence of "history," but not history in the sense of defining the lim-its or boundaries of a period, but history as that which remains to be written or composed—as that which "*will have been done.*"[32] The episode is not understood as an isolated period, where a cer-tain genre of discourse, as Lyotard says, comes to an end and another, different one, succeeds and goes beyond the former. Instead the episode is a point of transition in constant transforma-tion, where "the generations precipitate themselves."[33]

To understand phenomenology as an episode in Lyotard's thought, to grasp the episodic character of thinking, writing, act-ing, painting, creating in whatever form, in terms of beginnings and ends (*arché* and *telos*) is to assume certain rules or principles that delimit the scope of "phenomenology" or "philosophy" can be and have been already determined in advance of the perfor-mance. It is to presume a certain *truthfulness* of a particular method. In the end, it is to assign an axiomatic quality to its dis-courses and declarations. No such truths can be associated, in principle, with phenomenology in Lyotard's text. Indeed, Lyotard's own commitments to phenomenology, insofar as they are expressed, recall several announcements made by Husserl in 1911 and 1935 respectively:

> ...we must take phenomena as they turn this way or that, transforming themselves, according as the point of view or mode of attention changes in one way or another.[34]

And:

> Thus the philosopher must always have as his purpose to master the true and full sense of philosophy, the totality

of its infinite horizons. No line of knowledge, no individual truth must be absolutized [and isolated].[35]

To reiterate an earlier point then: the truths of phenomenology, of any philosophical stance, can be known only through the
experiences of its performance—of having been carried out. So,
according to its own desires, according to its historical presence
and conditions, according to its own "essential" variations, the
truths and meanings of phenomenology lie before it, never yet
fully articulated, at best only profiled. In this respect, is the phenomenologist at work in *Phenomenology* not in the position of
the philosopher described in "Answering the Question: What is
Postmodernism"?

The text he writes, the work he produces are not in principle governed by preestablished rules, and they cannot
be judged according to a determining judgment, by
applying familiar categories to the text or to the work.
Those rules and categories are what the work of art itself
is looking for.[36]

Here the philosopher, the artist, the writer is situated in the
interval. Here the episodes reign: it is constant state, a "nascent
state."[37] This is the postmodern condition of philosophy, of
knowledge, according to Lyotard. There are no rules binding
philosophic inquiry. There are no predetermined rules, categories, or practices governing the domain of critique. The
philosopher questions the determinations already supplied and
seeks others; the philosopher is always on the alert for such
truths. But more importantly, this condition is an episode the
philosopher is already *in the midst;* it is a variation of the phenomenological suspension of prejudices and presuppositions
articulated by Husserl, as Lyotard notes in *Phenomenology:*

In this sense the reduction is already by itself, as the
expression of the freedom of the pure ego, the revelation
of the contingent character of the world (49).

Such is the true significance of the "putting in parentheses": it turns the gaze of consciousness back on itself,
changes the direction of this gaze, and, in suspending the

world, lifts the veil which separates the ego from its own truth. This suspension shows that the ego remains what it is—that is, interlaced with the world—and that its concrete content remains the flux of *Abschattungen* across which the thing is drawn (51).

Perhaps, more appropriately at this point, it can be said that this phenomenological episode is the condition of the postmodern conceived too soon? Perhaps the phenomenological reduction, the parenthetical suspension of engagement, is the postmodern differend thought differently, conceived otherwise, under different conditions? Perhaps it can be said here that the conflict of episodes is the constant state of differends? Here the conflict between suspension and involvement that resounds throughout the histories of phenomenology would be the constant state of always beginning, of always grasping the necessity of making links. Here the modern is always becoming and already post; at its borders, which are forever changing, it is the post. And in this nascent state or condition, the post is always and already becoming modern, fixed, happy, consoled.

Indeed, this internal strife can be known only in terms of the impossibility of the complete reduction. Because "the ego remains...interlaced with the world," in the zone of the phenomenological suspension, where differends have been disengaged, the philosopher is always and already on alert. He or she is without rules, without a specified or stipulated way of making connections. The philosopher is always caught in the midst of "a constant flow of 'profiles' or 'perspectives' (*Abschattungen*)" (47), always caught between the lines of the mundane and the philosophic. The philosopher, in this case Lyotard, is always enveloped in the episodic. In this sense, the philosopher-phenomenologist seeks to find ways to put into phrases "something which should be able to be put into phrases" but which "cannot be phrased in the accepted idioms."[38] This persistent want of a link, the realized necessity of a phrase, of a power to restore signifying, is noted by Lyotard, at the outset of *Phenomenology*. Phenomenology can be grasped if one seeks its differends; phenomenology "can only be fixed if one investigates its interior" (32). Because there are no criteria, because there are no truths of phenomenology, in principle, to be articulated in advance of this experience, there is also "no knowledge of [the] practice." Does this mean that "one must judge case by case"?[39]

It is just this question that remains interminably open. It is just this question that constantly presents phenomenology *or* the postmodern *or* the differend in terms of "performance" in Lyotard's texts—the "constitutive experience" in which one always "knows" or "recalls" that to think the contingency of a *fact* is "to think that it belongs to the essence of the fact that it could be otherwise" (41). But this alignment of episodes—phenomenology, the postmodern, and the differend—is not meant to settle or resolve their differences. On the contrary, it is meant to notice and accommodate their heterogeneity. In Lyotard's text it is not an issue of having to choose between the adequacies of phenomenology, psychoanalysis, Marxism, deconstruction, and whatever else. One cannot decide with any finality or certainty, but one does decide for particular purposes, within particular contexts. Each episode is an introduction to a different sequence of *hodos* or ways of inquiring and experimenting. As Lyotard notes in his analysis of the debate surrounding phenomenology as a "third way," as an alternative to idealism and materialism or psychologism and objectivism, each episode, each perspective, each suspension of engagement, always "engages history [or whatever, one would suppose] in a new way and opens up a new future" (131).[40]

Each case is different. *Phenomenology* knows this. It knows that it must deny itself one possibility: "the possibility of settling, on the basis of its own rules, the differends it examines…"[41] Each case is affected differently by the play of contingency and fact—relativity. And in the midst, where one is only working with signs and never the things themselves, one must embrace the disquietude of ambiguity, multiplicities, and the heterogeneity of differends, realizing the necessity of having to begin, once again, engaging history in new ways. Moreover, if one is *always and already* beginning, and beginning is the constant state for the philosopher, then the task—indeed, the infinite task—of the philosopher is to resist the temptation to declare a "third way," a "third language," which mediates or transcends the heterogeneity of possible multiplicities that might be indicated from a particular standpoint (cf. 123–32). This much is clear for Lyotard: from the Lyotard who "describes" *Phenomenology* to the Lyotard who "reports" the *postmodern condition.* There is no way, no idiom, no discourse, no genre, no narrative technique, for Lyotard, that can resolve the crisis of making decisions, of rendering judgments on a case-by-case basis. Such is the condition for recollection; for soliciting philosophy, that is to say, for seeking to eliminate philosophy "as a separated existence."

Notes

1. Jean-François Lyotard, *Peregrinations: Law, Form, Event* (New York: Columbia University Press, 1988), 8–9. For a general overview of *Peregrinations,* see my review in *The Journal of Aesthetics and Art Criticism* 48, no. 1 (1990): 88–90.

2. Jean-François Lyotard, *La Phénoménologie* (Paris: Presses Universitaires de France, 1986), 10th edition. *Phenomenology* first appeared in 1954 and has been revised through many of its subsequent editions which have appeared in 1956, 1959, 1961, 1964, 1967, 1969, 1976, 1982, and 1986. Subsequent references to Lyotard's *Phenomenology* will appear in parentheses in the text.

3. To be sure, "radical reflection" or the "radical" return to the "things themselves" or "radical self-investigation" are notions and phrases central and common to the various epochs of phenomenology. But this is not to say these concepts are repeated always in identical ways. From Marx to Merleau-Ponty, through Husserl, Heidegger, and Sartre, the notion of the *radical* has undergone severe alterations.

On the one hand, for instance, there is Edmund Husserl's well-known claim, in "Philosophy as Rigorous Science," that "philosophy, however, is essentially a science of true beginnings, or origins, of *rizomata panton.*" See "Philosophy as Rigorous Science," in *Phenomenology and the Crisis of the Philosophy,* translated with an introduction by Quentin Lauer (New York: Harper and Row, 1965), 146. And there is his appeal to Descartes's *Meditations on First Philosophy* in the "Introduction" to the *Cartesian Meditations,* where Husserl turns toward Descartes to support his own attempt to articulate "The necessity of a radical new Beginning of philosophy" (sections 1 and 2).

Husserl begins: "Every beginner in philosophy knows the remarkable train of thoughts contained in the *Meditations*. Let us recall its guiding idea. The aim of the *Meditations* is a complete reforming of philosophy into a science grounded on an absolute foundation" (section 1).

On the other hand, for example, there is Maurice Merleau-Ponty's latter appeal, in "Marxism and Philosophy," *Sense and Non-Sense,* translated, with a preface, by Hubert L. Dreyfus and Patricia Allen Dreyfus (Evanston: Northwestern University Press, 1964), to Karl Marx's claim made in "A Contribution to The Critique of Hegel's 'Philosophy of Right'," *Critique of Hegel's 'Philosophy of Right',* edited with an introduction by Joseph O'Malley (Cambridge: Cambridge University Press, 1977). Marx states that "to be radical is to grasp matters by the root. But for man the root is man himself" (137). Merleau-Ponty writes:

> In particular, this subject is no longer alone, is no longer consciousness in general or pure being for itself. He is in the midst of other consciousnesses which likewise have a situation; he is for others, and because of this he undergoes an objectivation and becomes generic subject. *For the first time since Hegel, militant philosophy is reflecting not on subjectivity but on intersubjectivity.* Transcendental subjectivity, as Husserl pointed out, *is* intersubjectivity. Man no longer appears as a product of his environment or an absolute legislator but emerges as a product-producer, the locus where necessity can turn into concrete liberty.... Fortunately, with or without Husserl, the truth is dawning upon those who love philosophy (134 and 136; ellipses added).

For a more recent discussion and general assessment of these themes, and particularly how they pertain to recent issues involved in the dialogue between hermeneutics and the social sciences, see Calvin O. Schrag, *Radical Reflections and the Origins of the Human Sciences* (West Lafayette, Indiana: Purdue University Press, 1980).

4. This theme pervades Lyotard's analysis in this work and later works as well. In *Phenomenology* though, it is a theme announced from the interstices of phenomenology, and most particularly from those junctures where the influences of Hegel, Marx, Husserl, Merleau-Ponty, and Trân Duc Thao are most clearly pronounced. A provisional indexing of specific textual sites where the "matrix of intersubjectivity" is discussed in detail would alert the reader to the following pages: 43, 46–47, 53, 57, 59, 75–76, 80, 89, 100–101, 103, 106, 130, 134–136..

5. Cf. Edmund Husserl, *Experience and Judgment: Investigations in a Genealogy of Logic,* translated by James S. Churchill and Karl Ameriks, revised and edited by Ludwig Langrebe (Evanston: Northwestern University Press, 1973), 361–62.

6. Cf. Jean-François Lyotard, "Note sur les sens de 'post-'," *Le Postmoderne expliqué aux enfants* (Paris: Éditions Galilée, 1986), 126.

7. In this context, and I think throughout the various patterns developed in Lyotard's works, anámnesis can be likened to, should I say "is a variation of," a metaphor used by Husserl to announce the search for origin as the essence of philosophy: the "return to the things themselves," the "recovery" of or the "uncovering" the sedimentation of meaning—the "reawakening of basic experience," as Merleau-Ponty phrases it. This "return" is a retracing, a rethinking, a recurrence, a reawakening of paths, past *and* future.

8. I am appropriating a line Lyotard makes with respect to Merleau-Ponty because it seems to reflect his own intellectual penchants. In *Phenomenology* Lyotard says: "And if Merleau-Ponty returns to Marx's famous formula—'We cannot eliminate philosophy without realizing it'—it is because phenomenology seems to signify for him a philosophy *made real,* a philosophy eliminated as a separated existence" (136).

9. Jean-François Lyotard, *The Postmodern Condition: A Report on Knowledge,* translated by Geoff Bennington and Brian Massumi (Minneapolis: University of Minnesota Press, 1984), 53.

10. See Geoffrey Bennington, *Lyotard: Writing the Event* (New York: Columbia University Press, 1988), 1. There are two interrelated points to observe with respect to Bennington's analysis. First, Bennington offers only scant reference and discussion of *Phenomenology.* He writes that "the early work on phenomenology (*La Phénoménologie* (1953) [sic.]) is criticized and displaced in *Discours, figure* (1971), which argues for the predominance of a certain psychoanalysis over phenomenology." This is Bennington's only reference to *Phenomenology,* although there are several elaborate discussions of certain phenomenological themes as they appear in some of Lyotard's later writings, especially with respect to Lyotard's examinations of Marxism, psychoanalysis, and semiotics. Secondly, because *Phenomenology* is "criticized and displaced in *Discours, figure*" does not mean that its thematics and problematics—its differends as it were—are not undergoing some rethinking and reformulation by Lyotard. Moreover, to leave *Phenomenology* on these grounds is to neglect altogether its rather subtle

attempts to demonstrate the pertinence of phenomenology, as Lyotard construes it in this text, to the "political" issues in which many French intellectuals, including Lyotard, were engaged before and after 1954. (For Lyotard's account of his own "political" situation surrounding 1954 see "A Memorial for Marxism: For Pierre Souyri," in *Peregrinations: Law, Form, Event,* especially 45–75.)

This latter point is addressed by Vincent Descombes in *Modern French Philosophy,* translated by L. Scott-Fox and J.M. Harding (Cambridge: Cambridge University Press, 1980), 61, n. 12. About *Phenomenology* Descombes writes: "This short introduction to phenomenology is a significant document which well illustrates the preoccupation of the fifties. The interest of phenomenologists has shifted from mathematics to the human sciences, from the anti-historicist polemic to the search for a common ground with Marxism." Of course, Descombes's comments present other concerns, especially related to the "search for a common ground with Marxism." As is well known, some phenomenologists, at various moments Sartre and Merleau-Ponty are the most notorious examples, sought such a common ground in this regard. Others, such as Trân Duc Thao, to whom Lyotard refers frequently in his text, attempted to integrate phenomenology with Marxism in a critical manner to overcome what were perceived as intolerable contradictions and inconsistencies in the Husserlian version of phenomenology, especially at that point where Husserl turns toward history. See Trân Duc Thao, *Phenomenology and Dialectical Materialism,* translated by Daniel J. Herman and Donald V. Morano (Dordrecht and Boston: D. Reidel Publishing Company, 1986), 121–30 and 133–42.

11. Gilles Deleuze refers to this line from *Hamlet* in *Kant's Critical Philosophy: The Doctrine of the Faculties,* translated by Hugh Tomlinson and Barbara Habberjam (Minneapolis: University of Minnesota Press, 1984), vii. The exact reference is to *Hamlet,* act 1, sc. v, line 188.

12. Jean-François Lyotard, *The Differend: Phrases in Dispute,* translated by Georges Van Den Abbeele (Minneapolis: University of Minnesota Press, 1988), xiv.

13. As a preliminary guide, this introduction is not the place to undertake such a task, but an interesting internal comparison could be explored between Lyotard's conceptions of which of his works are "books of philosophy" or which are not. For example, *Phenomenology, Discours, Figure, The Postmodern Condition,* and *The Differend* are each identified as books of philosophy, in their respective ways. But

surely this is not to say that the conception of what constitutes "philosophy," or a "book," remains invariant throughout Lyotard's works.

14. Lyotard, *The Differend,* xiv.

15. The sequence of quoted phrases employed here can be found in several of Lyotard's works. See, for example, Jean-François Lyotard and Jean-Loup Thébaud *Just Gaming,* translated by Wlad Godzich, afterword by Samuel Weber (Minneapolis: University of Minnesota Press, 1985), 50–51; Lyotard *The Differend: Phrases in Dispute,* para. 36; Lyotard, *Peregrinations: Law, Form, Event,* 44; and Lyotard, "A Memorial for Marxism: For Pierre Souyri," *Peregrinations,* 49–50.

16. Although this is point made by Gilles Deleuze and Félix Guattari, in their *Kafka: Toward a Minor Literature,* translated by Dana Polan (Minneapolis: University of Minnesota Press, 1986), 28, it seems to mesh well with Lyotard's phenomenological exposé.

17. "Schizzes" or "schizzings" are terms derived from Gilles Deleuze and Félix Guattari, *Anti-Oedipus: Capitalism and Schizophrenia,* translated by Robert Hurley, Mark Seem, and Helen R. Lane (New York: The Viking Press, 1977), 243. For a exploration of how "schizzes" are incorporated into Lyotard's comprehension of the postmodern condition and the differend, see my "Postmodern *Différends,*" in *Crises in Continental Philosophy,* edited by Arleen Dallery and Charles Scott (Albany: State University of New York Press, 1990), 235–46.

18. Lyotard, *Peregrinations,* 6.

19. Ibid., 7

20. Maurice Merleau-Ponty, *Phenomenology of Perception,* translated by Colin Smith (London: Routledge and Kegan Paul, 1962), xii.

21. The remarks by Merleau-Ponty and Lyotard, in their respective ways, invoke images of Hegel's phenomenology of consciousness. Compare Merleau-Ponty's and Lyotard's comments to Hegel, when in the "Introduction" to *The Phenomenology of Mind,* translated by J. B. Baillie (New York: Harper and Row, 1967), he writes:

> The series of shapes, which consciousness traverses on this road, is rather the detailed history of the process of training and educating consciousness itself up to the level of science. That resolve presents this mental development (*Bildung*) in the simple form of an intended purpose, as immediately fin-

ished and complete, as having taken place; this pathway, on the other hand, is, as opposed to this abstract intention, or untruth, the actual carrying out of that process of development (136).

The goal, however, is fixed for knowledge just as necessarily as the succession in the process. The terminus is at that point where knowledge is no longer compelled to go beyond itself, where it finds its own self, and the notion corresponds to the object and the object to the notion. The progress towards this goal consequently is without halt, and at no earlier stage is satisfaction to be found. That which is confined to a life of nature is unable of itself to go beyond its immediate existence; but by something other than itself it is forced beyond that; and to be thus wrenched out of its setting is its death. Consciousness, however, is to itself its own notion; thereby it immediately transcends what is limited, and, since this latter belongs to it, consciousness transcends its own self. Along with the particular there is at the same time set up the "beyond," were this only, as in spatial intuition, *beside* what is limited. Consciousness, therefore, suffers this violence at its own hands; it destroys its own limited satisfaction (137–38).

22. Cf. Deleuze, *Kant's Critical Philosophy,* vii.

23. Lyotard, *The Postmodern Condition,* xxv.

24. Merleau-Ponty, *Phenomenology of Perception,* xxi.

25. Lyotard, *The Differend,* para. 93.

26. Ibid., para. 218.

27. Ibid.

28. Merleau-Ponty, *Phenomenology of Perception,* xx.

29. See Maurice Merleau-Ponty, *The Visible and the Invisible,* edited by Claude Lefort, translated by Alphonso Lingis (Evanston: Northwestern University Press, 1968), 130–55, but especially 155. The larger portion of the passage in question reads as follows:

And, in a sense, to understand a phrase is nothing else than to fully welcome it in its sonorous being, or, as we put it so well, to *hear what it says* (*l'entendre*). The meaning is not on the phrase like the butter on the bread, like the second layer of "psychic reality" spread over the sound: it is the totality of what is said, the integral of all the differentiations of the verbal chain; it is given within the words for those who have ears to hear. And conversely the whole landscape is overrun with words as with an invasion, it is henceforth but a variant of speech before our eyes, and to speak of its "style" is in our view to form a metaphor. *In a sense the whole of philosophy, as Husserl says, consists in restoring a power to signify, a birth of meaning, a wild meaning, an expression of experience by experience,* which in particular clarifies the special domain of language. And in this sense, as Valéry said, *language is everything, since it takes the voice of no one, since it is the very voice of things, the waves, and the forests. And what we have to understand is that there is no dialectical reversal from one of these views to the other; we do not have to reassemble them into a synthesis: they are two aspects of the reversibility which is the ultimate truth* (emphasis added).

30. Merleau-Ponty, *Phenomenology of Perception*, xiv.

31. Lyotard, *Peregrinations*, 2 and 8; see also 4.

32. Lyotard, "Answering the Question: What is Postmodernism?", translated by Regis Durand, *The Postmodern Condition*, 81.

33. Ibid., 79.

34. Husserl, "Philosophy as Rigorous Science," in *Phenomenology and the Crisis of Philosophy*, 109.

35. Edmund Husserl, "Philosophy and the Crisis of European Man," in *Phenomenology and the Crisis of Philosophy*, 181. This essay is otherwise known as "The Vienna Lecture," translated by David Carr as "Philosophy and the Crisis of European Humanity," in Edmund Husserl, *The Crisis of European Sciences and Transcendental Phenomenology* (Evanston: Northwestern University Press, 1970), see 291.

36. Lyotard, "Answering the Question: What is Postmodernism?", *The Postmodern Condition*, 81.

37. Ibid., 79.

38. Lyotard, *The Differend*, para. 93.

39. Cf. Lyotard and Thébaud, *Just Gaming*, 73–74.

40. Lyotard responds to a conflict that arises out of Georg Lukács's 1947 critique of Heidegger's and Sartre's existentialism. Lukács says, "It is important to note that modern phenomenology is

one of the numerous philosophical methods which seek to rise above both idealism and materialism by discovering a philosophical 'third way,' by making intuition the true source of knowledge." See Georg Lukács, "Existentialism," *Marxism and Human Liberation,* edited by E. San Juan, Jr. (New York: Dell Publishing, 1973), 245; see in general 244–51. For other brief discussions of this controversy see Mark Poster, *Existentialism in Postwar France: From Sartre to Althusser* (Princeton: Princeton University Press, 1975), 122–25; and Gregory Elliott, "Further Adventures of the Dialectic: Merleau-Ponty, Sartre, Althusser," in *Contemporary French Philosophy,* edited by A. Phillips Griffiths (Cambridge: Cambridge University Press, 1987), 196–97.

41. Lyotard, *The Differend,* xiv.

Translator's Acknowledgments

Thanks go to Marie-Hélène Remy, who tolerated countless interruptions of her work to answer my questions about French and weeded out my most embarrassing mistranslations; of course, I claim full credit for the errors that remain. Mark Tanzer provided valuable assistance in tracking down Heidegger citations, and Jeff Gaines offered similar help with Merleau-Ponty sources. Finally, thanks to Peter Ludlow for his constant encouragement and support of this project.

Phenomenology

Introduction

I.

"We will find the unity of phenomenology and its true meaning within ourselves," writes Merleau-Ponty, and Jeanson, for his part, emphasizes "the absurdity of demanding an objective definition of phenomenology." It is true that the meaning of this "movement," or "style," can only be fixed if one investigates its interior, taking upon oneself the question it bears; one would say as much of Marxism or Cartesianism. This signifies, in short, that philosophy must not only be grasped as event, and "from the outside," but worked through as thought—that is, as problem, genesis, give-and-take movement of thought. This constitutes the genuine objectivity that Husserl wanted; for the testimony of phenomenology does not lean in favor a simplistic subjectivism, such as Jeanson suggests, where the historian, in describing such thought, would in the final analysis simply inject his own opinions.

II.

Husserl's phenomenology germinated in the crisis of subjectivism and irrationalism at the end of the nineteenth and beginning of the twentieth centuries. We must situate this thought in history as it situated itself—in a history which is equally our own. It is *against* psychologism, *against* pragmatism, against an entire period of occidental thought that phenomenology has reflected, proceeded, and battled. It began, and remained, a meditation on knowledge, a knowledge of knowledge; and its famous "putting in parentheses" consists above all in dismissing a culture and a history, in tracing all knowledge back to a radical non-knowledge. But the rejection of this inheritance—of this "dogmatism," as Husserl somewhat peculiarly called it—is itself rooted in a heritage. Thus history envelops phenomenology, as Husserl knew from the beginning of his work to the end. Yet there is an ahistorical pretention in phenomenology; and this is why we will approach phenomenology through its history, and leave it in its debate with history.

III.

Phenomenology is comparable to Cartesianism, and one could certainly approach it adequately by such an angle: it is a logical meditation aimed at overflowing even the incertitudes of logic, by means of a language or logos excluding uncertainty. The Cartesian dream of a *Mathesis Universalis* is reborn in Husserl. It is clearly philosophy, then, and even post-Kantian philosophy since it wishes to avoid metaphysical systematization; it is a philosophy of the twentieth century, whose dream is to restore to this century its scientific mission by founding anew the conditions for its science. Realizing that knowledge is embodied in concrete or "empirical" science, it seeks the foundation of this scientific knowledge. This is the point of departure, the roots into which phenomenology inquires: the immediate data of knowledge. Kant had already investigated the a priori conditions of knowledge, but this a priori already prejudiced the solution. Phenomenology wishes to avoid even this hypostasis—thus its interrogative style, its radicalism, its essential incompletion.

IV.

Why "phenomenology"? The term signifies a study of "phenomena," that is to say, of *that* which appears to consciousness, *that* which is "given." It seeks to explore this given—"the thing itself" which one perceives, of which one thinks and speaks—without constructing hypotheses concerning either the relationship which binds this phenomena to the being *of which* it is phenomena, or the relationship which unites it with the I *for which* it is phenomena. One must not go beyond the piece of wax in doing a philosophy of extended substance, nor in doing a philosophy of the a priori spatial forms of sensibility; one must remain with the piece of wax itself, describe only what is given, without presuppositions. Thus a critical moment takes form at the heart of the phenomenological meditation, a "denial of science" (Merleau-Ponty) which consists in a refusal to proceed to explanation. For to explain the red of this lampshade is precisely to abandon it as *this* red spread out on this lampshade, under whose circle I am thinking of red; it is to set it up as a vibration of a given frequency and intensity, to set in its place "something," the object for the physicist which is not, above all, "the thing itself" for me. There is always a preflective, an unreflective, a prepredicative upon which reflection and science are based, and which these latter always conjur away when explaining themselves.

We see, then, the two faces of phenomenology: a strong faith in the sciences drives its program of solidly establishing their underpinnings, and of ultimately stabilizing their whole edifice and heading off a future crisis. But to accomplish this, it must leave even science behind, and plunge into matters "innocently." A rationalist bent leads Husserl to engage himself in the prerational; yet an imperceptible inflection can turn this prerationality into an irrationality, and phenomenology into a stronghold of irrationalism. From Husserl to Heidegger there is certainly an inheritance, but equally a mutation. Our exposé will not attempt to erase this ambiguity, inscribed as it is in the very history of the phenomenological school.

V.

It is above all with respect to the human sciences that phenomenological reflection claims our attention. This is no accident: in the investigation of the immediate data prior to all scientific thematization, and the justification of such, phenomenology lays bare the fundamental manner, or essence, of the consciousness of this data, which is intentionality. In place of the traditional consciousness which "digests," or at least ingests, the external world (as in Condillac, for example), phenomenology reveals a consciousness which "bursts outward" (Sartre)—a consciousness, in sum, which *is* nothing if not a relation to the world. Given the objective experimental methods, modelled after physics, that are used by psychology, sociology, etc., are these fields not radically inadequate? Will it not prove necessary at least to begin by laying out and making clear the diverse modes according to which consciousness is "interwoven with the world"? For example, having taken the social realm as object—which constitutes a decision of a metaphysical character—it is doubtless necessary to explain the meaning of the fact of "being-in-society" for consciousness, and consequently to interrogate this fact naively. Thus the inevitable contradictions which issue from the posing of the very sociological problem are liquidated: the phenomenological temptation is not to replace the sciences of man, but to focus their problematics, thus selecting their results and orienting their research. We will attempt to retrace this path.

VI.

Need we emphasize the importance of phenomenology? It is a step in "European" thought and has understood itself as such, as Husserl showed in the *Crisis*. We will have to fix its historical significance even though this is not ascribable once and for all, since there are presently *many* phenomenologists, and since its meaning is still 'in process', unfinished precisely because it is historical. There are, in effect, different 'accents' from Heidegger to Fink, from Merleau-Ponty to Ricoeur, from Pos or Thevanez to Levinas, which justify the prudence with which we will begin. Yet there remains a common phenomenological "style," as Jean Wahl has rightly noted; and, not being able here, except on occasion, to localize the finer or coarser divergences which separate these philosophers, it is this common style above all which we will seek to outline, after having rendered to Husserl that which is Husserl's: *having begun.*

I
Husserl

I.

The Eidetic

1. Psychologistic Scepticism

The psychologism against which Husserl battles identifies the subject of knowledge with the psychological subject. It insists that the judgment "This wall is yellow" is not a proposition independent of my expressing it and perceiving the wall. We could argue that "wall" and "yellow" are concepts definable by extension and intension independently of all concrete thought; is it necessary to accord them some existence in themselves transcending the subject and the real? The *contradictions* of realism concerning ideas (Platonism, for example) are inevitable and unsolvable. Yet if we admit the principle of *noncontradiction* as a criterion for the validity of a thesis (here, Platonism), do we not affirm its independence from concrete thought? We pass thus from the problem of the *material* of logic, the concept, to that of its organization, *the principles;* but psychologism is not disarmed on this new terrain: when the logician claims that two contrary propositions cannot be true simultaneously, he states only that it is impossible in fact, on the level of actual consciousness, to believe that the wall is yellow *and* that it is green. The validity of such general principles is based in my psychological organization, and if they are indemonstrable it is precisely because they are innate; from which it follows obviously that there is no ultimate truth independent of the psychological workings which drive it. How could I know if my knowledge is adequate to its object, as the classical conception of truth demands? What is the sign of this adequation? Necessarily, a certain "state of consciousness" by which all questions concerning the object of knowledge are found superfluous—subjective certitude.

Thus concepts become actual; principles become contingent conditions of psychological mechanisms; and truth becomes belief reinforced by success. Since scientific knowledge is itself relative to our organization, no law can be said to be absolutely true; it is simply a hypothesis in view of verification without end, and its validity is defined in terms of the efficacity of the operations that render it possible. Science thus weaves a network of useful symbols ("energy," "force," etc.) with which it dresses the world; its only objective is to establish constant relations among these symbols, permitting action. The question is not, properly speaking, about *knowledge of the world.* We cannot assert the progress of this knowledge in the history of science: history is a development without specifiable meaning, an accumulation of trials and errors. We must therefore renounce the posing of questions that science cannot answer. Finally, mathematics is a vast formal system of conventionally established symbols and operative axioms without restrictive content: all is possible in our imagination (Poincaré). Mathematical truth winds up being defined in reference to the axioms chosen from the outset. All these theses converge in scepticism.

2. Essences

Husserl shows (in the *Logical Investigations* and *Ideas I*) that this scepticism, resting as it does on empiricism, is its own contradiction. Basically, the assumption at the root of all empiricism is the claim that experience is the sole source of truth for all knowledge—but then this claim must rely, in turn, on the proof of experience. Yet experience, never furnishing more than the contingent and particular, cannot provide science with the universal and necessary principle of such an assumption. Thus, empiricism cannot be understood through empiricism. At the same time it is impossible to confuse, for example, the flux of subjective states experienced by the mathematician when he reasons, and reason itself, since the operations of reasoning are definable independently of this flux; we can only say the mathematician reasons rightly when by this subjective flux he rises to the objectivity of true reasoning. But this ideal objectivity is defined by logical conditions, and the truth of reason (its noncontradiction) *imposes itself* on the mathematician as it does on the logician. True reasoning is universally valid, while false reasoning is tainted by subjectivity, and thus untransmissible. Even a rectangular triangle possesses an ideal objectivity in the sense that it is the subject of a collection of predicates, inalienable on pain of *losing* the rectangular triangle itself. To avoid the ambiguity of the word "idea," we say that it possesses an *essence* constituted by all its predicates, whose negation would entail the negation of the triangle itself. For example, all triangles are, by their essence, convex.

Yet if we remain on the level of mathematical "objects," the formalist argument that views these objects as conventional concepts retains its force; one could hold, for example, that the supposedly "essential" characteristics of the mathematical object are in reality deducible from the start from the axioms. For this reason Husserl expands his theory of essences, in the second volume of *Logical Investigations,* to apply even to that favored ground of empiricism: *perception.* When we say "The wall is yellow," do we involve essences in this judgment? For example, can the color be grasped independently of the surface on which it is "spread out"? No, since a color separated from the space in which it is given would be unthinkable. If, in "varying" the color in the imagination, we withdraw its predicate "extended," we negate the possibility of the color itself, and so arrive at a *consciousness of impossibility;* this reveals the essence. In judgments there are, therefore, limits to our fantasying which are fixed for us by the judged *things themselves,* and which Fantasy itself discloses by means of variation.

The proceedings of imaginational variation give us the essence itself, the being of the object. The object (*Objekt*) is "anything whatsoever," for example the number two, the note C, a circle, any proposition or perceptible datum whatsoever (*Ideas I*). We perform the "variation" arbitrarily, obeying only the present and actual evidence of the "I can" or the "I cannot." The essence, or *eidos,* of the object is constituted by the invariant that remains identical throughout the variations. Thus if we operate the variation on the perceptible thing as object, we obtain the 'way of being' of any such thing: a spatio-temporal whole, endowed with secondary qualities and presented as substance and causal unity.

The essence is therefore experienced in an actual, concrete intuition. This "vision of essences" (*Wesenschau*) has nothing of a metaphysical character, nor is the theory of essences itself framed within a Platonic realism where the existence of the essence would be assumed; the essence is only that in which the "thing itself" is revealed to me in an *originary givenness*.

This involves a return "to the things themselves" (*zu den Sachen selbst*), a closing off of all metaphysical avenues. But the empiricists remained metaphysical in confusing this demand to return to the things themselves with the demand to found all knowledge on experience, taking as given, without question, that experience alone gives the things themselves—a pragmatist-empiricist prejudice. In reality, the ultimate source of justification for all rational assertions is in "seeing" (*Sehen*) in general, that is, in primordial dator consciousness (*Ideas I*). We have presupposed nothing, Husserl says, "not even the concept of philosophy." While psychologism wishes to identify the *"eidos"* obtained through variation with the "concept" of psychological and empirical origin, we reply simply that in so doing it says more than it realizes if it wishes to hold to the originary intuition that it pretends to take as its law. Perhaps the number two, as concept, is constructed from experience, but as I obtain this *eidos* number by variation, I claim that this *eidos* is "prior" to all theory about the construction of the number, and the proof of this is that all genetic explanation relies on the present knowledge of "something" which this genesis must explain. The empiricist interpretation of the formation of the number two *presupposes* the originary understanding of this number. This understanding is thus a precondition for all empirical science; while the *eidos* it yields us is only a pure possibility, there is a priority to this possibility with respect to the real which concerns science.

3. Eidetic Science

Here it proves possible to grant this science its validity. The incertitudes of science—perceptible already in the human sciences, but reaching ultimately even to those which act as models, namely physics and mathematics—have their source in a blind concern for experimentation. Before doing physics one must study the essence of the physical fact; the same applies, of course, to the other disciplines as well. From the definition of the *eidos* grasped by originary intuition, we can draw methodological conclusions that orient empirical research. It is already clear, for example, that no serious empirical psychology can be undertaken if the essence of the psychological has not been grasped in a manner avoiding all confusion with the essence of the physical. In other words, we must define the eidetic laws that guide all empirical knowledge: this study constitutes the general eidetic science or ontology of nature (that is, the study of being or essence). This ontology has been grasped in its truth, as prolegomenon to the corresponding empirical science, in the development of geometry and the recognition of the role it plays in the purification of knowledge in physics. All natural things have spatial being as their essence, and geometry is the eidetics of space; but it does not encompass the entire essence of the thing, nor the scope of other disciplines. We should thus make hierarchical distinctions, beginning with the empirical: (1) material essences (that of clothing, for example) studied by ontologies or sciences of material eidetics; (2) regional essences (for example, cultural objects) directing the former and explicating by regional eidetics; and (3) the essence of the object in general, according to the previously given definition, which is studied by a formal ontology.[1] This last essence, which directs all the regional essences, is a "pure eidetic form," and the "formal region" which it determines is not a region coordinated with material regions, but the "empty form 'region' in general." This formal ontology is identifiable with pure logic; it is the *Mathesis Universalis,* the goal of Descartes and Leibniz. Clearly this ontology must define not only the notion of theory in general, but all the possible forms of theories (the system of multiplicities).

Such is the first great movement of the Husserlian process. It rests upon the fact, defined as "the individual and the contingent"; the contingency of the fact is related to the necessary essence, since to think of its contingency is to think that it belongs to the essence of the fact that it could be otherwise. Fac-

---

1. The hierarchy is obviously a network, not linear in form.

ticity thus implies a necessity. This process apparently restates Platonism and its "naivité." But it also contains Cartesianism, since it strives to present the knowledge of essences not as the end of all knowledge, but as the necessary introduction to knowledge of the material world. In this sense the truth of the eidetic is the empirical, and this is why the "eidetic reduction," by which we are invited to pass from the contingent facticity of the object to its intelligible contents, can still be called "mundane." To each empirical science there corresponds an eidetic science concerning the regional *eidos* of the objects studied, and phenomenology itself is, at this stage of Husserlian thought, defined as the eidetic science of the region consciousness; in other words, in all the empirical human sciences (*Geisteswissenschaften*) we find an essence of consciousness necessarily involved, and it is this implication that Husserl attempts to articulate in *Ideas II*.

The Transcendental

1. The Problematic of the Subject

Phenomenology thus assumed the role of propaedeutic to the "human sciences." But in the second volume of *Logical Investigations* a reaction develops that leads us into philosophy proper. Once understood, the "problematic of correlation"—that is, the group of problems posed by the relationship between thought and its object—reveals the question that forms its nucleus: subjectivity. It is probably here that the influence exercised by Brentano on Husserl, Brentano's student, is most strongly felt, for the key observation of Brentano's psychology was that consciousness is always *consciousness of something*—that is, that consciousness is intentionality. If we transpose this theme to the eidetic level, it signifies that any object—thing, concept, the *eidos* itself, whatever—is an object for some consciousness, and it becomes necessary to describe the manner in which I know the object, and in which the object exists for me. Does this return to psychologism? While it might seem so, this is not in fact the case.

The concern to radically ground knowledge led Husserl to formal eidetics, that is, to a sort of logicism. But in moving beyond this system of essences two paths are open: either to develop the science of logic as *Mathesis Universalis,* that is, to constitute a science of sciences *on the side of the object;* or, on the contrary, to pass to an analysis of the meaning, *for the subject,* of the logical concepts used by this science, the meaning of the relations it establishes between these concepts, and the meaning of the truths which it seeks to establish. In short, to question knowledge itself, not in order to construct a "theory," but to found even more radically the radical eidetic knowledge. In taking consciousness as already in the simple givenness of the object, there was an implicit correlation of ego and object which had to lead back to an analysis of this ego; thus, Husserl chose the second path. The radicality of the *eidos* presupposed a more fundamental radicality. Why? Because the logical object itself can be given to me confusedly or obscurely, because I then have of such laws and relations "a simple representation" which is empty, formal, and operative. In the sixth of the *Logical Investigations* Husserl shows that logical (or categorial) intuition goes beyond this simple symbolic comprehension only when "founded" on sensible intuition. Does this amount to a return to the Kantian thesis that the concept without intuition is empty? The Neo-Kantians thought so.

Thus, in the second volume of the *Logical Investigations* we note two interwoven movements, of which the first, in introducing the analysis of actual experience as the foundation of all knowledge, seems to return to psychologism; while the second, in basing the clear comprehension of the ideal object on the intuition of the sensible thing, seems to return phenomenology to the Kantian position. Of these positions, Husserl chooses the latter, and the "realism" of essences appears to slide into an idealism of the subject: "The analysis of the value of logical principles leads to research centered on the subject" (*Formal and Transcendental Logic*). It seems at this point that we need only choose between an idealism centered around the empirical ego and a transcendental idealism of a Kantian sort; yet neither can satisfy Husserl. The first fails because it renders incomprehensible the true propositions that are reduced in psychologism to nonpriviledged states of consciousness, as well as because it lumps together in the same flux of consciousness that which is valuable and that which is not—thus destroying science, and itself as universal theory. The second is insufficient in that it only explains the a priori conditions of pure knowledge (pure mathematics or physics), but not the real conditions of concrete knowledge: the transcendental Kantian "subjectivity" is simply the set of all conditions governing *all possible objects in general,* the concrete ego is dismissed to the sensible level as object (this is why Husserl accuses Kant of psychologism), and the question of how real experience enters the a priori realm of all possible knowledge, in order to permit the elaboration of particular scientific laws, remains unanswered—in the same way that in the *Critique of Practical Reason* the integration of real moral experience into the a priori conditions of pure morality remains impossible by Kant's own admission. Husserl thus preserves the idea of a truth founded on the subject of knowledge, but rejects the separation of this subject from the concrete subject. It is at this stage that he encounters Descartes.

2. The Reduction

It is in the *Idea of Phenomenology* (1907) that the Cartesian inspiration appears; it continues in *Ideas I* and again, in a lesser way, in the *Cartesian Meditations*. The Cartesian subject obtained through the doubt and the *cogito* is a concrete subject, a lived reality, not an abstract framework. At the same time, this subject is an absolute—this is, indeed, the point of the first two meditations: it is self-sufficient, it has no need of anything on which to found its being. The perception this subject has of itself "is and remains, for as long as it lasts, an absolute, a 'this', something which is in itself what it is, something which acts as a standard by which I can measure what 'being' and 'being given' can and must signify" (*Idea of Phenomenology*). The intuition of experience by itself constitutes the model of all originary evidence. And in *Ideas I,* Husserl retraces the Cartesian movement which begins with the perceived or natural world. There is nothing surprising in this "shift" from the logical plane to the natural plane: both are "mundane," and the object in general is as much a thing as a concept. There is not, properly speaking, a shift, but an accentuation, and we must understand fully that the reduction applies in general to *all transcendence* (that is to say, to all things in themselves).

The natural attitude contains a thesis or implicit position by which I *find the world there* and accept it as existing. "Corporeal objects are simply there for me in some spatial distribution; they are 'present', in a literal or figurative sense, whether or not I pay special attention to them.... Living beings equally, and perhaps men, are there for me in an immediate way.... Real objects are there for me, determinate, more or less known, along with objects actually perceived, without themselves being perceived or even present in an intuitive fashion.... But the totality of these objects, co-present in intuition in a clear or obscure, distinct or indistinct manner, and constantly covering the present field of perception—even this does not exhaust the world which is there for me in a conscious way in each waking instant. On the contrary, it extends without limit according to a fixed order of beings, and is partly overlapped and partly surrounded by an *obscurely apprehended horizon of indeterminate reality....* This misty horizon, incapable of ever being totally determinate, is necessarily there.... The world...has its temporal horizon infinite in both directions, its past and its future, the known and the unknown, immediately living and void of life. [Ultimately this world is not only] a world of things, but with the same immediacy a world of values, a world of goods, a practical world" (*Ideas I,* sect. 27). But this world also contains an ideal realm: if I am presently engaged in doing arithmetic, this arithmetical world is there for me, though different from the natural world in that it is there for me only insofar as I assume the role of mathematician, while natural reality is always already there. Finally, the natural world is also the world of intersubjectivity.

The natural thesis, implicit in the natural attitude, is that by which "I discover [reality] as existing and receive it, as it gives itself to me, equally as existing" (*Ideas I,* sect. 30). I can, of course, put in doubt something given in the natural world; deny the "information" which I receive; distinguish, for example, that which is "real" from that which is "illusion," etc.; but this doubt "changes nothing about the general position of the natural attitude" (ibid.). Such doubt avails us a more "adequate" and "rigorous" grasp of this existing world than is given us in immediate perception, and allows scientific knowledge to go beyond perception; but in this knowledge the intrinsic thesis of the natural attitude is preserved, since there is no science which does not posit the existence of the real world of which it is a science.

This allusion to Descartes's first two meditations shows that no sooner is the Cartesian radicalism taken up again than Husserl reveals its inadequacy. The Cartesian doubt bearing on the natural object (for example, the piece of wax) remains in itself a mundane attitude, is nothing but a *modification* of this attitude, and so does not meet the profound demand for radicality. A proof of this is given in *Cartesian Meditations,* where Husserl denounces the geometric prejudice by which Descartes assimilates the cogito to an axiom of knowledge in general, when in fact the cogito must be much more since it is the foundation even of axioms. This geometric prejudice reveals the inadequacy of doubt as a method of radicalization. To this doubt we must therefore oppose an attitude by which *I take no position with respect to the world as existing,* whether this position be natural assumption of existence, Cartesian doubt, etc. In fact, of course, I, as empirical and concrete subject, continue to participate in the natural attitude toward the world—"this thesis is still a lived reality"—but I make no use of it. It is suspended, put out of play, out of circulation, between parentheses; and by this "reduction" (or *"epoché"*) the surrounding world is no longer simply existing, but "phenomena of being" (*Cartesian Meditations,* sect. 8).

3. The Pure Ego

What is the result of this reductive operation? Insofar as the concrete ego is interwoven with the natural world, it is clear that it is itself reduced; in other words, I must abstain from all theses concerning the self as existing. But it is no less clear that there is an *I,* who properly abstains, and who is the I even of the reduction. This I is called the *pure ego,* and the *epoché* is the universal method by which I grasp myself as pure ego. Does this pure ego have content? No, in the sense that it is not a container; yes, in the sense that it is an aiming at something. But is it not necessary to apply the reduction to this content? Before answering this question, it is only right to note that at first glance the reduction fully dissociates, on the one hand, the world as totality of things, and on the other, the conscious subject of the reduction. We must proceed to eidetically analyze the region thing and the region consciousness.

The natural object—for example, that tree there—is given to me in and by a constant flow of profiles or perspectives (*Abschattungen*). These perspectives, throughout which the object is profiled, are experiences relating to the object by their sense of apprehension. The object exists as a "same" which is given to me throughout the continual modifications, and what makes it a thing for me (that is, in itself for me) is precisely the necessary inadequacy of my grasp of the object. But this idea of inadequacy is equivocal: since the object is profiled throughout successive perspectives, I have access to it only unilaterally, through one of its sides; but at the same time I am given the other sides of the object, not "in person," but suggested by the side given sensorially. In other words, the object as it is given to me in perception is always open on the horizons of indetermination, "it indicates in advance a diversity of perceptions of which the phases, in passing continually from one to another, blend into the unity of a perception" (*Ideas I*, sect. 44). Thus the object can never be given as an absolute, there being "an indefinite imperfection resulting from the insupressible essence of the correlation between thing and perception of thing" (ibid.). In the course of perception the successive profiles are altered, and a new perspective of the object can come to correct an earlier one; there is no contradiction here—since the flux of all these perspectives merges into the unity of one perception—but only the object emerging throughout these alterations without end.

By contrast, the experience itself is given to itself in an "immanent perception." Self-consciousness gives the experience in itself, that is, taken as an absolute. This does not mean that experience is always adequately grasped in its full unity: since it is a flux, it is always already distant, it has already passed when I wish to grasp it. This is why it is only as *retained* experience, as retention, that I can grasp it, and why "the total flux of my experience is a unity of experience which is in principle impossible to grasp by perception, by letting ourselves completely 'flow with' it" (ibid.). This particular difficulty, which is at the same time an essential problematic of consciousness, extends into the study of internal time consciousness;[1] but even though there is no immediate adequation of consciousness with itself, the fact remains that *all experience bears in itself the possibility in principle of its*

---

1. See part 2, chapter 4, sect. 2.

existence. "The flux of experience which is my flux, that of the thinking subject, can be as large as one likes, unapprehended and unknown as regards parts already past and yet to come; nonetheless, I need only look on this life as it flows in its real presence and grasp myself in this act as the pure subject of this life, to be able to say necessarily and without restriction: *I am, this life is, I live—cogito*" (*Ideas I,* sect. 46).

Consequently, the first result of the reduction is to oblige us to dissociate sharply the mundane or natural in general from the nonmundane subject; but in pursuing the description we end up in some way hierarchizing these two regions of being in general: we conclude, in effect, with the *contingency* of the object (taken as the model of the mundane) and the *necessity* of the pure ego, the residue of the reduction. The thing and the world in general are not apodictic (cf. *Cartesian Meditations*) since they do not exclude the possibility of being doubted, and thus do not exclude the possibility of their nonexistence; the totality of experience (in the Kantian sense) can prove to be simple appearance, nothing more than a coherent dream. In this sense the reduction is already by itself, as the expression of the freedom of the pure ego, the revelation of the contingent character of the world. By contrast, the subject of the reduction—the pure ego—is evident to itself in apodictic evidence, which signifies that the flow of experience that constitutes it as it appears to itself cannot be put in question either in its essence or its existence. This apodicticity does not imply an adequation; the certitude of the being of the ego does not guarantee the certitude of the knowledge of the ego. But it suffices to oppose the transcendent perception of the thing and of the world in general to immanent perception: "The position of the world, which is a 'contingent' position, opposes itself to the position of my pure ego and my egological experience, which is a 'necessary' and absolutely indubitable experience. Any object given 'in person' could equally well not exist, while any experience given 'in person' could not fail to exist" (*Ideas I,* sect. 46). This law is a law of essence.

We had wondered: must the phenomenological reduction apply to the contents of the pure ego? We realize now that this question implies a radical misunderstanding, which Husserl imputes even to Descartes: it amounts to treating the subject as an object (*res cogitans*). The pure ego is not a thing, *since it is not given to itself in the way an object is given to it.* It does not "peacefully cohabit" with the world, any more than it has need of the world to be; for if we imagine that the world were annihilated (we recognize in this passage the technique of imaginary variations fixing the essence) "the being of consciousness would certainly be necessarily modified..., but it would not be undermined in its own existence." In effect, an annihilated world would only signify for the consciousness living this world the disappearance, in the flow of its experiences, of certain orderly empirical connections, this carrying off with it certain rational connections ordered after the former. But this annihilation does not imply the exclusion of other experiences and other connections between experiences. In other words, "no real being is necessary for the being of consciousness itself. Immanent being is thus indubitably an absolute being, in that *nulla 'res' indiget ad existendum.* On the other hand, the world of the transcendent *res* refers itself entirely to a consciousness— not to a consciousness conceived of logically, but to an actual consciousness" (*Ideas I,* sect. 49).

In *Ideas I* the *epoché* thus takes on a double significance: for the one part negative, in that it isolates a consciousness as phenomenological residue—and it is at this level that the eidetic (that is, still natural) analysis of consciousness operates; for the other part positive, since it causes consciousness to emerge as absolute radicality. With the phenomenological reduction the Husserlian program of an indubitable and originary foundation is realized on a new level—for the eidetic radicality brings us to a *transcendental* radicality, that is, to a radicality upon which all transcendence is founded (recall that by transcendence we mean the mode of presentation of an object in general). We asked how a mathematical or scientific truth could be possible, and contra scepticism we saw that it is possible only by the positing of the essence of what is thought; this positing of the essence required nothing but a "seeing" (*Schau*), and the essence was grasped in an originary givenness. Then in meditating on this givenness itself, and more precisely on the originary givenness of things (in perception), we discovered, beneath the attitude by which we are given things, a consciousness whose essence is heterogeneous to all that given in consciousness—that is, all transcendence—

and by which the very meaning of the transcendent is posited. Such is the true significance of the putting in parentheses: it turns the gaze of consciousness back on itself, changes the direction of this gaze, and, in suspending the world, lifts the veil that separates the ego from its own truth. This suspension shows that the ego remains what it is—that is, interlaced with the world— and that its concrete content remains the flux of *Abschattungen* across which the thing is drawn. "The concrete contents of subjective life do not disappear in the passage to the philosophical dimension, but are revealed there in their authenticity. The positing of the world has been 'put out of action', but not annihilated: it remains alive, though in a 'modified' form which permits consciousness to be fully aware of itself. The epoché is not a logical operation demanded by the conditions of a theoretical problem, but a process providing access to a new mode of *existence:* transcendental existence as absolute existence. Such significance can only be realized in an act of freedom."[2]

4. Pure Ego, Psychological Ego, Kantian Subject

There cannot, therefore, be any question of a return to psychologistic subjectivism, since the ego revealed by the reduction is precisely not the natural psychological or psychophysical ego; nor does it do any good to reply from a Kantian position, since the transcendental ego is not "a consciousness conceived of logically, but an actual consciousness."

1) We cannot confuse the transcendental ego with the psychological ego, as the *Cartesian Meditations* insist. Certainly, Husserl says, "I am the ego, which remains in the natural attitude, and at the same time the transcendental ego. But I can only take account of this by way of the phenomenological reduction." The empirical ego is "interested in the world," and it lives there entirely naturally; on the basis of this ego the phenomenological attitude constitutes a *doubling of this ego* which establishes the

---

2. Trân Duc Thao, *Phénoménologie et Matérialisme Dialectique* (Mihn-Tan, 1951), pp. 73–74. I cannot recommend this remarkable little book too strongly to the reader.

disinterested spectator, the phenomenological ego. It is this ego of the disinterested spectator that looks into the phenomenological reflection, undertaken itself through a disinterested attitude of the spectator. We must therefore admit simultaneously that the ego in question *is* the concrete ego, since there is no difference of content between psychology and phenomenology, and that it is *not* the concrete ego, since it is disengaged from its being in the world. Intentional psychology and transcendental phenomenology both begin with the *cogito,* but the first remains on the mundane level, while the second develops its analysis from the transcendental cogito which envelops the world in its totality, including the psychological ego.

2) Do we find ourselves, then, before the Kantian transcendental subject? Many passages, as much in *Ideas I* as in the *Cartesian Meditations,* suggest this, and it is not by chance that the Neo-Kantian Natorp declared himself in agreement with *Ideas I.*[3] These suggestions stem above all from Husserl's insistence on the absolute being of consciousness, meant to head off the belief that this ego is no more than a region of nature (which is a tenet even of psychology). He shows on the contrary that nature is not possible except for the ego: "Nature is possible only under the aspect of an intentional unity motivated in consciousness by means of immanent connections.... The domain of experience as absolute essence...is by essence independent of all being pertaining to the world, to nature, and does not require even these for its existence. The existence of nature cannot condition the existence of consciousness, since nature manifests itself as the correlate of consciousness" (*Ideas I,* sect. 51). Resting on this transcendental philosophy, the Neo-Kantians (Natorp, Rickert, Kreis, Zocher) showed that, for Husserl as for Kant, objectivity leads to the totality of these a priori conditions, and that the main phenomenological problem is the same as that of the *Critique:* how is a *datum* possible? As for the intuitionist aspect, and especially this pure grasp of experience by itself in immanent perception, there could be no doubt for Kreis that its origin lay in an empiricist prejudice. How, in effect, could it be

---

3. "Husserls Ideen zu Einer Reinen Phänomenologie," *Logos* VII, 1917–18.

that a subject which is nothing but the a priori conditions of all possible objectivity, could also be an empirical flux able to grasp its radical indubitability in an originary presence to itself? Kant wrote: "Outside of the logical significance of the ego, we have no knowledge of the subject in itself which is the basis of the ego, as of all thoughts, having the quality of a substratum." The Husserlian principle of immanence, resulting as it does in an empiricist psychology, is incompatible with the constitution of objectivity. But setting these reservations aside, Husserl would be a good Kantian.

In a famous article,[4] Eugen Fink, then assisting Husserl, responds to these commentaries in a manner which clarifies our problem: phenomenology does not, properly speaking, pose the Critical problem, but the problem of *the origin of the world,* the very problem posed by religion and metaphysics. This problem is no doubt eliminated by Critical philosophy, because it was always posed and resolved in aporetic terms. Kantianism has replaced it with the question of the conditions of possibility of the world for me. But these conditions are themselves mundane, and all Kantian analysis remains only at the eidetic (that is, mundane) level. It is thus clear that Critical philosophy commits an error in its interpretation of phenomenology. This error is particularly evident concerning the question of immanence and the "fusion" of the transcendental subject with the concrete subject. In reality there is no fusion, but on the contrary a doubling; for the unity of the subject is given prior to all conceptual construction. What is incomprehensible in Critical philosophy in general is that the system of a priori conditions for objectivity should be a subject, the transcendental subject. In reality it is the perceiving subject itself who constructs the world, though it is in this world through its perception. When we explore this subject from the point of view of its interwovenness with the world, in order to distinguish it from the world, we use the criterion of immanence; but the paradoxical situation here is that even the contents of this immanence are nothing other than the world as aimed at, as intentional, as phenomena—and so, as this world is posited as really existing and

---

4. "Die Phänomenologische Philosophie E. Husserls in der Gegenwartigen Kritik," *Kantstudien* XXXVIII, 1933; cosigned by Husserl.

transcendent by the ego. The reduction leading out of this paradox permits us precisely to grasp how there is for us a thing in
itself, that is, how the transcendence of the object can have the
sense of transcendence in the immanence of the subject. The
reduction gives the subject its truth as constituent of transcendence, the truth implicit in the alienated attitude that is the natural attitude.

5. Intentionality

If the object can have a sense of transcendence at the very
heart of the ego's immanence, this is, properly speaking, because
there is no immanence in consciousness. The distinction between
immanent data and transcendent data, on which Husserl bases the
first separation of consciousness and world, is still a mundane distinction. In reality, the phenomenological *epoché* discloses an
essential characteristic of consciousness which clarifies the above-
mentioned paradox. For intentionality is not only that psychological datum which Husserl inherited from Brentano, but that which
makes possible the *epoché* itself: perceiving this pipe on the table
is not, as the associationists thought, having a reproduction of this
pipe in miniature *in* the mind, but *to intend* the object pipe itself.
In putting out of play the natural doxa (the spontaneous positing
of the existence of the object), the reduction reveals the object as
intended, as phenomenon; the pipe is, then, nothing but a *vis-à-vis*
(*Gegenstand*), and my consciousness that for which there is a vis-
à-vis. My consciousness cannot be thought if we imaginarily take
away what it is consciousness of; we cannot even say that it would
then be consciousness of nothing, since this nothing would at once
be the phenomenon of which there would be consciousness.
Imaginary variation operated on consciousness thus reveals that
its proper being is to be consciousness *of* something. It is because
consciousness is intentionality that it is possible to effect the
reduction without losing what is reduced. To reduce is, at bottom,
to transform all data into vis-à-vis, into phenomena, and so reveal
the essential characteristics of the I: the radical or absolute foundation, the source of all significance and constitutive power, the
connection of intentionality with its object.

Of course, intentionality is not simply a perceptual characteristic. Indeed, Husserl distinguishes various types of intentional
acts: imaginations, representations, experiences of other people,
sensory and categorial intuitions, receptive and spontaneous
acts, etc.—in brief, all the contents of the Cartesian enumera-
tion: "What am I, this ego that thinks? A thing which doubts,
understands, conceives, affirms, denies, wants or does not want,
imagines and feels." Elsewhere Husserl distinguishes the actual I
in which there is "explicit" consciousness of the object, from the
nonactual I in which consciousness of the object is implicit, or
"potential." The actual experience (for example, the act of atten-
tive grasping) is always encircled by a field of inactive experiences, and "the flux of experience can never be constituted by
pure actualities" (*Ideas I,* sect. 35). All experiences, actual or
inactual, are equally intentional. One must not confuse intentionality with attention, as there is inattentive, or implicit, intentionality. We will have occasion to return to this point, so essential is it for psychological science; for it contains the entire
phenomenological thesis concerning the unconscious.

We see, therefore, that we can speak, with Husserl, of an
inclusion of the world *in* consciousness, since consciousness is
not only the I-pole (or *noesis*) of intentionality, but equally the
object-pole (or *noema*); but we must make clear that this inclusion is not *real* (as when the pipe is in the room), but intentional
(the pipe phenomena is for consciousness). This intentional
inclusion, revealed in each particular case by the method of
intentional analysis, shows that the relationship of consciousness
to its object is not that of two exterior and independent realities.
For on the one hand, the object is a *Gegenstand,* a phenomenon,
leading back to the consciousness to which it appears; while on
the other hand, consciousness is consciousness of this phenomenon. It is because the inclusion is intentional that it is possible to ground the transcendent in the immanent without detract-
ing from it. Thus intentionality is itself an answer to the
question, "How can there be an object in itself for me?" To perceive the pipe is precisely to see it as really existing. The meaning of the world is therefore decoded as the meaning that I give
to the world, though this meaning is experienced as objective, I
discover it; otherwise it would not be the meaning which the

world has for me. In putting *intentional analysis* in our hands, the reduction permits us to describe rigorously the subject-object relationship. This description consists in putting to work the "philosophy" immanent in natural consciousness, not in espousing the data passively. Yet this "philosophy" is the very intentionality which defines it. Intentional analysis must (as its name suggests) therefore clarify how the meaning of the object's being is *constituted;* for while intentionality is an "aiming at," it is also a giving of meaning. Intentional analysis lays hold of the constituted object as meaning and reveals this *constitution.* Thus in *Ideas II* Husserl proceeds successively to the constitutions of material nature, living nature, and Spirit. It follows from this that subjectivity is not "creator," since it is in itself nothing but *Ichpol;* but "objectivity" (*Gegenstandlichkeit*) exists for its part only as the pole of an intentional aiming which gives it its meaning of objectivity.

III

The "Lifeworld"

1. Transcendental Idealism and Its Contradictions

At this stage we return, it seems, to a "transcendental idealism" (*Cartesian Meditations*); and this transcendental idealism was loaded into the very enterprise of the reduction. But since the transcendental subject is not different from the concrete subject, transcendental idealism appears, moreover, obliged to be a solipsism. I am alone in the world, this world is in itself nothing but the *idea* of the unity of all objects, the thing is nothing but unity of my perceptions of the thing, that is, the *Abschattungen*— all meaning is grounded "in" my consciousness as giver of meaning (*Sinngebung*). In reality Husserl never rested with this monadic idealism—first, because the experience of objectivity leads back to the agreement of a plurality of subjects, and second, because the other person is himself given to me in an absolutely originary experience. Other *egos* "are not simply representations and represented objects in me, synthetic unities of a process of verification unfolding itself within me, but rightly 'others'" (*Cartesian Meditations,* sect. 42). The otherness of the Other distinguishes itself from the simple transcendence of the thing in that the Other is an ego for himself, and his unity lies not in my perception but in himself; in other words, the Other is a pure ego that needs nothing in order to exist, an absolute existence and a radical point of departure for himself, as I am for myself. The question then becomes: how can there be a constituting subject (the Other) for a constituting subject (myself)? Of course, the Other is experienced by me as a "stranger" (*Cartesian Meditations*) since he is a source of meaning and intentionality. But beneath this experience of strangeness (which will provide Sartre with his themes of the separation of consciousness-es), on the transcendental level, the explication of the Other cannot be spelled out in the same terms as the explication of the thing; yet for all that, to the extent that the Other exists for me, he equally exists through me, if we are to believe the essential results of the transcendental reduction. This demand for an explication of the Other is not truly met in the *Cartesian Meditations,* the very text from which we drew our formulation of the above-stated problem. In effect, after having described "the assimilating apperception" by which the Other's body is given to me as his lived body—thus suggesting the psychic as its proper index—and after having made his "indirect accessibility" our foundation for the existence of the Other, Husserl declares that from the phenomenological point of view "the Other is a modification of 'my' ego" (*Cartesian Meditations,* sect. 52)—thus disappointing our expectations. In *Ideas II,* part 3, Husserl makes up for this by underlining the opposition between "natural world" and "world of the spirit (*Geist*)," and the absolute ontological priority of the latter over the former; the unity of the thing is that of the deployment of its *Abschattungen* for a consciousness, while the unity of the person is the "unity of absolute manifestation." In the case of the subject, and by consequence the Other as subject (that is, as *alter ego*), we cannot *reduce* the real existence to an intentional correlate, since what I intentionalize when I see the Other is precisely an absolute existence: here, being real and being intentional merge together. We can thus posit separately a "community of persons," which Ricoeur[1] likens to Durkheim's collective consciousness or the objective spirit in a Hegelian sense, and which is at the same time constituted by the mutual grasp which the subjectivities and the community have of their environment. This community of persons is constitutive of its own world (the medieval world, the Greek world, etc.), but is it originarily constitutive? To affirm this would be to claim that the transcendental and solipsistic subject is not *radical,* since it has sunk its roots into a world of the spirit, in a culture which is itself constitutive.

---

1. In "Analyse et Problemes dans Ideen II," *Revue de Metaphysique et de Morale,* 1951.

In other words, transcendental philosophy as philosophy of the subject fails to integrate a cultural sociology; rather, there remains a "tension" between them (Ricoeur), perhaps even a contradiction, and one not grafted onto phenomenological thought, but inherent in it. For it is transcendental philosophy itself which leads to the problem of intersubjectivity or the community of persons, as is shown by the parallel paths of the *Cartesian Meditations* and *Ideas.* It is clear that the cultural sociological viewpoint already present in *Ideas II,* and largely dominating the last writings (the *Crisis* and the letter to Levi-Bruhl), introduces, by Husserl's own admission, something like a *historical relativism*—the very thing which transcendental philosophy fought against. Yet for all that, this philosophy can neither avoid leading into the problem of the Other, nor elaborate this problem in a way which revises the acquisitions of radical subjectivism. With the intentional analysis of the Other, the radicality is no longer on the side of the ego, but on the side of intersubjectivity; and this latter is not simply an intersubjectivity for the ego—the affirmation by which ego would restore the ego's position as unique foundation—but an absolute intersubjectivity, or if one prefers, a *first* intersubjectivity. But Husserl himself never went this far: the radicality of the transcendental *cogito,* as it is established in *Ideas I,* remains the core of all his philosophy. In section 2 of the *Crisis,* for example, we find this significant criticism leveled against transcendental Cartesianism: Descartes "did not realize that all distinctions of the type I and You or within and without are only 'constituted' in the absolute *ego."* Thus the you, like the that, is nothing but a synthesis of egological experiences.

Still, it is in the direction of this "cultural sociology" that Husserl's thought evolved toward the end of his life. The *Crisis*—of which only the first two parts were published, in 1936 in Belgrade—testifies to this fully. Husserl is careful to link this reflection on history—that is to say, on intersubjectivity—closely to his own problem of transcendental radicality: "This work attempts to base the ineluctible necessity of a conversion—that from philosophy to transcendental phenomenology—on the path of a teleologico-historic coming-to-consciousness, applied to the origins of our critical situation as it concerns science and philosophy. This work constitutes, then, an independent introduction to

transcendental phenomenology." In other words, the path followed up to now, which led us from logico-mathematical or perceptual problems to the absolute *ego*—this path is not privileged;
the way of history is equally sure. The elucidation of history in
which we are engaged clarifies the task of philosophy. "We who
not only have a spiritual heritage, but are through and through
beings becoming according to the historical spirit—it is only by
this title that we have a task which is truly ours" (*Crisis,* sect. 15).
Philosophy cannot pass history by, because philosophy concerned with radicality must understand and go beyond the
immediate historical data which are in reality the sedimentations
of history, the prejudices, and which constitute its "world" in a
cultural sense. Yet what is the crisis before which we finds ourselves? It is the crisis issuing from objectivism. It is not, properly
speaking, a crisis of theoretical physics, but the crisis reaching to
the meaning of the sciences for life itself. What characterizes the
modern spirit is logico-mathematical formalization (the very
thing which constituted the hope of the *Logical Investigations*)
and the mathematization of natural knowledge: Leibniz's *Mathesis Universalis* and Galileo's new methodology. It is on this basis
that objectivism develops: in discovering the world as applied
mathematics, Galileo recovered it as the work of consciousness
(*Crisis,* sect. 9). Thus objectivist formalism alienates: this alienation appeared as malaise when objective science lays hold of
the subject; for we are then forced to choose between construing
the psychological after the model of physical, or renouncing any
rigorous study of the psychological. Descartes announced the
solution in introducing the *transcendental motif:* by the *cogito,*
the truth of the world as phenomena, as *cogitatum,* is restored,
and the objectivist alienation leading to the metaphysical aporia
of the soul and God are brought to an end—or at least would be
brought to an end, if Descartes had not himself been taken in by
Galilean objectivism, and had not consequently confused the
transcendental *cogito* with the psychological ego. The thesis of
the *ego res cogitans* counteracts the entire transcendental effort.
Thus the double Cartesian heritage: the metaphysical rationalism that eliminates the *ego,* and the sceptical empiricism that
destroys knowledge. It is only transcendentalism—articulating
all knowledge on a fundamental ego, which is the giver of mean-

ing, and lives a pre-objective, prescientific life in an immediate "lifeworld" of which science is only the veneer—which will give objectivism its true foundation and take away its power to alienate. Transcendental philosophy makes possible the reconciliation of objectivism and subjectivism, abstract knowledge and concrete life. Thus the fate of European humanity, which is also that of humanity in general, is linked to the possibility of converting philosophy to phenomenology: "We are by our philosophical activity the functionaries of humanity."

2. The Lifeworld

We cannot here prolong our description of Husserl's evolution in this direction. We can see that, since the doctrine of the *Wesenschau,* the accentuation of his thought was noticably modified; yet it is nonetheless incontestable that this thought remained, to the end, on an axis whose main problem was radicality. But the absolute *ego,* which the *Ideas* made into a unique, identical, and universal pole, appears in a new light in the philosophy of the last period. We have just seen it engaged in history and intersubjectivity. Husserl sometimes called it *Leben* ("life"), the subject of the *Lebenswelt;* and while we knew already that there is ultimately no difference between the concrete ego and the transcendental subject, the identification is here underlined to the point that the last aspect of Husserl's philosophy could be characterized as empiricist (Jean Wahl).

Lebenswelt philosophy is primarily engaged in the elaboration of the great question posed in *Logical Investigations:* what is meant by "truth"? It is clear that truth cannot be defined here as adequation of thought with its object, since any such definition implies that the philosophy defining this truth must contemplate both all thoughts and all objects in their relation of total exteriority; and phenomenology has taught us that any such exteriority is unthinkable. But truth can no more be defined as a body of a priori conditions, since this body (or transcendental subject, in a Kantian sense) cannot say "I," is not radical, is in fact nothing but an objective moment of subjectivity. Truth can only be defined as lived experience of truth—this is evidence. Yet this experience is not simply a sentiment, for it is clear that sentiment provides no guarantee against error; evidence is the originary mode of intentionality, the moment of consciousness where the thing is said to be given in flesh and blood to consciousness, where the intuition is "filled." In order to answer the question "Is the wall yellow?" I either enter the room and look at the wall (originary evidence, on the perceptual level, which Husserl often called simply "experience"), try to remember, or ask others. In these latter two cases, I check whether there exists in myself or someone else an "experience," still present, of the color of the wall. All possible justification of a judgment must pass through this "present experience" of the thing itself; thus evidence is the meaning of all justification, or of all rationalization. Of course, experience does not apply only to the perceptual object, but equally to value (for example, beauty)—in brief, to any of the intentional modes enumerated above.

In any case, this evidence or experience of the truth does not provide a total guarantee against error. No doubt there are cases where we do not have the experience that we speak of, and we test it ourselves against evidence; but error can creep into the evidence itself. This yellow wall, when seen in the light of day, is grey. There are thus two successive and contradictory pieces of evidence, the first of which contained an error. To which Husserl replies, in *Formal and Transcendental Logic,* section 8: "Even evidence given as apodictic can be revealed as illusion; it presupposes, nonetheless, evidence of the same kind, at whose hands it is 'exploded'." In other words it is always exclusively in present experience that the earlier experience appears illusory to me. Thus there is not some "true experience" towards which we must turn, like some index of truth and error. Truth is always and exclusively tested in present experience, and the flux of experience cannot be relived; we can say only that if such experience is presently given to me as past and erroneous evidence, this actuality itself constitutes a new "experience" expressing, in the living present, the past error and the present truth as the correction of that error. There is no absolute truth, as postulated by dogmatism and scepticism alike; rather, truth defines itself in process, as revision, correction, and self-surpassing—this dialectical operation always taking place at the heart of the living present (*lebendige Gegenwart*). Thus, contrary to a dogmatic thesis, error is comprehensible, since it is implied in the very meaning of the evidence by which consciousness constitutes the truth. We therefore respond correctly to the question of truth by describing the experience of the true and insisting on the genetic development of the ego: truth is not an object but a movement, and it exists only if this movement is *actually carried out by the ego.*

Consequently, in order to verify a judgment—that is, to explain the meaning of truth—we must proceed to a regressive analysis leading to a precategorial (prepredicative) experience which constitutes a fundamental presupposition of logic in general (Aron Gurwitsch[2]). This presupposition is not a logical axiom, but a philosophical condition of possibility, constituting the ground (*Boden*) into which all predication sinks its roots. Prior to any science, its subject matter is pregiven to us in a passive "belief," and the "passive, universal pregiven of all judging activity" is termed "world," "the absolute, independent substratum, in the strong sense of absolute independence" (*Experience and Judgment*). The radical foundation of truth reveals itself in the end as a return to the *Lebenswelt* through intentional analysis, and at the heart of this world the constituting subject "receives things" as passive syntheses prior to all exact knowledge. "This receptivity must be viewed as an inferior stage of activity" (ibid.), signifying that the transcendental ego constituting the meaning of these objects refers implicitly to a passive grasp of the object, to a complicity with the object. This too-short allusion permits us to specify finally that the "world" in question here is obviously not the world of natural science, but the totality or idea, in a Kantian sense, of all there is, and everything of which there can be consciousness.

Thus, after the reduction that shattered the world in its constituted form—in order to grant the constituting ego its authenticity as giver of meaning—the Husserlian project, in exploring the meaning of this subjective *Sinngebung,* recovers the world as the very reality of the constitutor. It is obviously not the same world: the natural world is a fetishized world where the subject

---

2. "Presuppositions Philosophiques de la Logique," *Revue de Metaphysique et de Morale,* 1951.

abandons himself as naturally existing and naively "objectifies" the meaning of objects. The reduction seeks to efface this alienation, and the primordial world it discovers is the ground of the lived experiences on which the truth of the theoretical consciousness is based. The truths of science are founded neither in God, as Descartes thought, nor on the a priori conditions of possibility, as Kant thought, but on the immediate experience of evidence by which individual and world find themselves in harmony from the beginning.

Note on Husserl and Hegel

It is from Hegel that the term phenomenology received its full and singular meaning, with the 1807 publication of *Die Phänomenologie des Geistes*. Phenomenology is "science of consciousness," "in that consciousness is, in general, knowledge of an object, either exterior or interior." Hegel writes in the preface to the *Phenomenology:* "The immediate Being of spirit, *consciousness,* possesses two moments: that of knowledge, and that of objectivity which is the negative with regard to this knowledge. When spirit develops itself in this element of consciousness and displays its moments, this opposition occurs at each particular moment, and they all therefore appear as faces of consciousness. The science of this path is the science of the *experience* had by consciousness" (*Phenomenology of Spirit,* preface, sect. 36). There is thus no answer to the question whether philosophy must begin with the object (realism) or with the ego (idealism). The very idea of phenomenology puts this question out of play: consciousness is always consciousness of, and there is no object which is not an object *for.* There is no immanence of the object to consciousness unless one correlatively assigns the object a rational meaning, without which the object would not be an object for. Concept or meaning is not exterior to Being; rather, Being is immediately concept in itself, and the concept is Being for itself. The thinking of Being is Being thinking itself; consequently, the method this thought employs—philosophy itself—is not constituted by a body of categories independent of what is thought, of its contents. The form of thought is distinguished from the content only formally: it is, concretely, the content itself which grasps itself, the in-itself becoming for-itself. "We must consider the forms of thought in itself and for itself; for they are the object and the activity of the object" (*Encyclopedia*). Thus the Kantian error—while a positive error, as a moment in the

Spirit's coming-to-truth—consisted in discovering the forms and categories as the absolute foundation of the thought of the object and the object for thought: the error of admitting the transcendental as originary.

According to the dialectical identification of Being and concept, the problem of originality is in effect "passed over": there is no absolute and immediate beginning—i.e., something without consciousness, or a consciousness without an object—at the very least because the concept of an immediate or beginning contains as its dialectical negation the perspective of a subsequent progression, a mediation. "The progression is not superfluous; it would be so only if the beginning was already truly absolute" (*Science of Logic*). Nothing is absolute, all is derived, to the point that the only "nonderived" reality is the whole of the system of derivations—that is, the absolute Idea of the *Logic* and the absolute Knowledge of *Phenomenology;* the result of the dialectical mediation appears to itself as the only immediate absolute. Absolute knowledge, writes Hyppolite, "does not start from an origin, but from the very movement of starting, from the *minimum rationale* which is the triad *Being-Nothingness-Becoming;* that is, it starts from the Absolute as mediation, in its immediate form of becoming."[1]

This double Hegelian proposition—that Being is already meaning and that there is no origin which founds knowledge— permits a clear distinction between the Husserlian and Hegelian positions, apart from their common criticism of Kant. With the first part of this proposition, Husserlian phenomenology is effectively in agreement: the object is "constituted" by the sedimentation of meanings, which are not the Kantian a priori conditions of all experience, since the understanding which establishes these conditions as the foundation of all experience is itself already founded on experience. There is no logical priority of categories, nor even of the forms by which a transcendental subject is given objects; on the contrary, as Husserl showed in *Experience and Judgment,* judgments and the categories they employ presuppose a first certitude, that there is being—that is to say,

---

1. *Logique et Existence: Essai sur la Logique de Hegel* (PUF, 1953), p. 85.

the belief in a reality. Husserl calls it *Glaube*—faith, belief—to emphasize that it acts as a preknowledge. Before all predicative activity, even before all givenness of meaning, and there even if it concerns the perception of the sensible thing, there is at the heart of the "passive presentation" "*a practiced and ineluctible faith* in the existence of *some* reality...the source of all knowledge and exercised in itself, [this belief] is not entirely recovered in a properly spoken and explicit knowledge" (Waelhens).[2]

If the recovery of the totality of the real (in the Hegelian sense) is thus claimed impossible, it is precisely because there is an originary, immediate, and absolute reality that grounds all possible recovery. Must we then say that is *ineffable,* if it is true that all logos, all rational discourse, all dialectic of thought presupposes in its turn the originary *faith*? Is there thus some prerationality here? We can see that this question sharply distinguishes Hegel from Husserlian and post-Husserlian phenomenology. "There is not for Hegel," writes Hyppolite, "an ineffable which would be before or beyond knowledge, no immediate singularity or transcendence; there is no ontological silence but rather, in the dialectical discourse, a progressive conquest of meaning. This does not imply that this meaning would rightly be prior to the discourse that discovers and creates it...but that the meaning develops itself in this very discourse."[3] In the article *Glauben und Wissen* Hegel had already attacked the transcendence of the Kantian in-itself as the product of a "philosophy of the understanding," for which the presence of the object remains the simple appearance of a *hidden* reality. Yet, does Husserl not introduce another, similar transcendence in *Experience and Judgment* in the form of the pre-predicative *Lebenswelt*? Insofar as this originary lifeworld is prepredicative, all predication and discourse certainly implies it, but equally lacks it, and cannot properly say anything about it. Here again, though in a different sense, *Glauben* replaces *Wissen,* and the silence of faith puts an end to all of man's dialogue concerning Being. From here the truth about Husserl would be found in

---

2. *Phénoménologie et Vérité* (PUF, 1950), pp. 52, 50.
3. *Logique et Existence,* pp. 25–26.

Heidegger, for whom "the duality of the ego and Being is insurmountable" (Waelhens), and for whom the pretended absolute
knowledge simply manifests the "metaphysical," speculative, and
inauthentic character of the system that it assumes. Husserl's
immediate origin is for Hegel something mediated which does
not see itself as a moment in the total becoming of Being and
Logos; but Hegel's Absolute, as Becoming taken as totality closing back in upon itself and for itself in the person of the Sage, is
for Husserl itself founded and nonoriginary, speculative, and not
the "ground" of all possible truth.

Consequently, when Kojève claims, in the *Introduction à la
Lecture de Hegel,* that the method of the *Phenomenology of
Spirit* is the same as Husserl's, "purely descriptive and non-
dialectical,"[4] he is no doubt right. But we must add, for all that,
that the Hegelian phenomenology *closes* the system, it is the
total recovery of total reality in absolute knowledge, while
Husserlian description *inaugurates* the grasping of the "thing
itself" before all predication; this is why the latter never finishes
correcting itself, erasing itself, since it is a battle of language
against itself aimed at attaining the originary (one might note
here the remarkable similarities—all things being equal—
between the styles of Merleau-Ponty and Bergson). In this battle
the defeat of philosophy, of logos, is certain, since the originary,
once described, is as described no longer originary. In Hegel, on
the contrary, immediate being, that pretended "origin," is
already logos, meaning, not the achievement of regressive analysis or the absolute beginning of existence; we cannot "consider
the beginning as an immediate, but as mediated and derivative,
since it is itself determined vis-à-vis the determination of the
later result" (*Science of Logic*). "No object, insofar as it presents
itself as something external to and remote from reason, as independent of it, can resist it, nor in the face of it be particular in
nature, nor avoid being penetrated by it" (ibid.).

Apparently, then, the conflict is complete between Husserl
and Hegelian rationalism. If nonetheless we consider that the
phenomenological enterprise is fundamentally contradictory as

---

4. *Introduction à la Lecture de Hegel,* p. 467.

designation in language of a prelogical signified in being, it is forever unachieved precisely because it is dialectically turned back from Being to meaning, by way of intentional analysis; thus truth is becoming, and not simply "actual evidence." It is a taking back and correction of successive evidence, a dialectic of evidence. As Merleau-Ponty writes, "'The truth' is another name for sedimentation, which is itself the presence of all 'presents' in our own";[5] truth is *Sinngenesis,* genesis of meaning. At the same time, if we admit that "the *Phenomenology of Spirit* is militant philosophy, not yet triumphant" (Merleau-Ponty), if we view Hegelian rationalism as open, the system as a step, then perhaps Husserl and Hegel finally converge on the position, "We wish to see the true in the form of result" of the *Philosophy of Right*—but on condition that this result also be a moment.

---

5. "Sur la Phénoménologie du Langage," in *Eloges de la Philosophie et Autres Essais* (Gallimard, 1960), p. 109.

Part II

Phenomenology and the Human Sciences

The Relation of Phenomenology
to the Human Sciences

Clearly the problem of the human sciences is not brushed aside in phenomenological thought; on the contrary, we might say that in a sense it is at the center. It is in view of psychologism, sociologism, and historicism that Husserl attempts to restore validity to science in general, and to the human sciences in particular. Psychologism pretends to reduce the conditions for true knowledge to actual psychological conditions, such that the logical principles guaranteeing this knowledge are themselves guaranteed only by factual laws established by the psychologist. Sociologism seeks to show that all knowledge can be systematically deduced from the elements of the social milieu in which it is elaborated. And historicism, in emphasizing the relativity of this milieu to historical developments, puts the finishing touches on this degradation of knowledge: in the final analysis each civilization, and within each civilization each historical period, and within each period each individual consciousness, produces an architecture of myths, spells out a *Weltanschauung*. This "worldview" is best expressed in philosophy, religion, and art, but ultimately even science is a "worldview." The German philosopher Dilthey, whose influence on Husserl was considerable, is at the center of this relativist philosophy.

Relativism is born of the human sciences (in Comte's positivism, Schiller's humanism, and James's pragmatism), and leads to their destruction as sciences. For if we destroy the validity of knowledge in subordinating its foundational logical principles and categories (e.g., causality) to psychological processes discovered by the psychologist, the question arises as to the validity of the principles and categories used by the psychologist to estab- lish this process. To make psychology the key science is to destroy it as science, since it is incapable of legitimating itself. In other words, relativism attacks not only the natural sciences, but the human sciences, and even further the logical infrastructure on which all science is based. It is in defense of this infrastructure that Husserl so lucidly begins his work.

From this perspective, phenomenology is a logic: from the *Logical Investigations* to *Experience and Judgment,* we can see the continuity of Husserlian thought. But this logic is neither formal nor metaphysical: it does not satisfy itself with a set of operations and operatory conditions defining the field of true reasoning; but neither does it want to base the operatory on the transcendent, nor to hold that two plus three equals five because God wishes it, or because the God who put this equation within us cannot be a deceiver. The logic which is phenomenology is a foundational logic that investigates how *in fact* there is truth for us: experience, in the Husserlian sense, manifests this fact. This cannot amount to an empiricism pure and simple, whose profound contradictions Husserl has often criticized. In reality, it attempts to extract the justification out of the fact. Does this fall back into sceptical relativism? No, since relativism—psychologism, for example—fails precisely to draw out the value of reality: it reduces the necessary to the contigent, and the logical truth of the judgment to the psychological certitude experienced by the individual who judges. What phenomenology tries to do, on the contrary, is, beginning with the true judgment, to descend again to what is *actually experienced* by the individual who judges. Yet in order to grasp what is actually experienced, one must adhere to a description that closely follows the modifications of consciousness: the concept of certitude proposed by Mill, which describes truth as an experience of consciousness, fails absolutely to take account of what is really experienced. Thus arises the necessity of an extremely fine and supple description of consciousness, whose working hypothesis is the phenomenological reduction: in effect, this recaptures the subject in its subjectivity by extracting it from its alienation in the heart of the natural world, and guaranteeing that the description holds of actually experienced consciousness, rather than of some more or less objectivated substitute for it. For the psychologist there are no true or false judgments, only judgments to be described. The truth of what the subject judges to be observed is for the psychologist only one more event, in no way privileged; the judging subject is determined, bound up in the series of motivations that bear responsibility for the judgment. Thus, we can reach the experience of truth which is to be described only if we do not eliminate the subject of the experience from the outset.

The philosophy of the transcendental subject therefore ineluctably required a *psychology* of the empirical subject. We have long insisted on the identity of the two subjects. From the perspective of the human sciences, this identity signifies that "intentional psychology already bears in itself the transcendental" (*Cartesian Meditations*), or that psychological description, properly performed, ultimately cannot fail to restore the constituent intentionality of the transcendental ego. Phenomenology was thus led inevitably to write psychology into its program, not only because it poses particular methodological problems, but above all because phenomenology is a philosophy of the *cogito*.

The link that unites it to *sociology* is no less intimate: we noted very briefly, concerning the fifth *Cartesian Meditation* and *Ideas II,* how transcendental solipsism runs up against the problem of the Other. Husserl does not seem to have settled on a definite version of this problem. Still, when he writes that "transcendental subjectivity is intersubjectivity," or that the spiritual world has an absolute ontological priority over the natural world, we are led to believe that the *Einfühlung,* or coexistence with the Other which is an understanding of the Other, brings about a relation of reciprocity where the concrete transcendental subject grasps itself as Other in that it is "an other" for the Other, and introduces an absolutely original element into the problematic of this subject: the social. Here again phenomenology was led inevitably, by the very fact that it is not a metaphysics but a philosophy of the concrete, to take hold of sociological data in order to clarify itself, and equally to put into question the procedures by which sociologists obtain this data, in order to clarify sociology.

It was the very inquiry of history into phenomenology, and

into all of philosophy, that led phenomenology to inquire into history. But it was equally the discovery, at the heart of the concrete transcendental subject, of the problem of time, which is also—considering the psycho-phenomenological "parallelism"— the problem of individual history: how can there be history for consciousness? This question is close enough to that of phenomenology: how can there be an Other for my consciousness? In effect, through history I become other in remaining the same; through the Other, an other is given as an I. In particular, if we define truth as experience of truth, and if we admit that experiences succeed one another in an infinite flux, the problem of internal time and of individual history is eminently capable of rendering obsolete any pretention to truth: one never steps foot twice in the same river, and yet truth seems to demand atemporality. If in the end transcendental subjectivity is defined as intersubjectivity, the same problem arises, no longer on the individual level, but on the level of collective history.

Phenomenology constitutes at the same time both a "logical" introduction to the human sciences, in seeking to define the object eidetically prior to all experimentation; and a philosophical "reprise" of the results of experimentation, insofar as it seeks to retreive fundamental meaning, particularly in proceeding to the critical analysis of the intellectual apparatus used. In one sense, phenomenology is the eidetic science corresponding to the empirical human sciences (especially to psychology); in another sense, it places itself at the heart of these sciences, at the heart of the fact, so realizing the truth of philosophy, which is to draw out the essence *in* the concrete itself: it is therefore the "revealer" of the human sciences. These two senses correspond to the two levels of Husserlian thought. They are thoroughly run together in current phenomenological thought, but we see that they can nonetheless be isolated, and that the eidetic definition (by imaginary variation) is difficult to use, not to say arbitrary.

V

Phenomenology and Psychology

1. Introspection

The objectivist psychologist, phenomenology's principal inter-locutor, holds that psychology must renounce any privileging of the ego in its knowledge of itself. Introspection as a general psychological method admitted *first of all* the axiom: conscious experience constitutes in itself a knowledge of consciousness. I am afraid, thus I know what fear is, since I have fear. This axiom in turn assumed that the conscious state is completely *transparent* to consciousness, and that all the facts of consciousness are facts for consciousness. In other words, experience gives itself immediately with its meaning, whenever consciousness turns itself toward it.

Secondly, introspective psychology conceived of this experience as *interiority:* we must distinguish categorically between exterior and interior, that is, between objective or natural science, and the subjective accessible only through introspection. This dissociation quickly proved difficult to follow, however, above all with the progress of psychology, for the problem arose as to *where* to draw the line of demarcation: from there followed parallelist and epiphenomenalist hypotheses, etc., until it was finally understood—with phenomenology playing a major role in this maturation of the problem—that a border can only separate regions of the same nature; yet the psychological does not exist in the same way as the organic.

Thirdly, conscious experience had a strictly *individual* character, in the double sense that it is the experience of a situated and dated individual, and that it is itself an experience which cannot be reproduced. This last feature was invoked by such "psychologists" in a decisive way to defend the introspective method: the experience must be grasped immediately, failing which the experience reflected upon *afterwards* may be a new experience—the link between the one and the other bearing no guarantee of fidelity. The heterogeneity of "conscious states" condemns any means of laying hold of them other than intro-spection. The individuality and even uniqueness of the experi-ence grasped by introspection clearly poses the double problem of its universality and its transmissibility. Traditional philosophy and introspective psychology generally resolved this first by hypothesizing a "human nature," a "human condition" that authorizes the universalization of particular results, and then by favoring as instrument of communication, rather than everyday or scientific language, an expressive language which would least betray interiority—hence the preference in this psychology for literary forms. We note here, in passing, one of the essential problems of Bergsonism which Bergson never confronted direct-ly, though it constitutes the key to all the others.

Finally, the heterogeneity of experiences in the flux of con-sciousness introduced a *contingency* which absolutely forbids that the psychologist elaborate psychological laws—for law pre-supposes determinism.

2. Reflection

Phenomenology finds itself in agreement with objectivism in criticizing certain introspectionist theses. The claim that the meaning of a content of consciousness is immediately manifest and graspable as such, is belied by the psychological enterprise itself: if we feel the need for a psychological science, it is precise-ly because we know that we don't know the psychological realm. It is true that in being afraid I have fear, but still I do not know *what* fear is, I "know" only *that* I have it; consider the distance between these two types of knowledge. In reality "knowledge of the self by the self is indirect, it is a construction, I must decode my behavior as I decode that of the other," (Merleau-Ponty).[1]

---

1. Merleau-Ponty, "Les Sciences de l'Homme et la Phénoménologie," in *Résumés de Cours, College de France 1952–60* (Gallimard, 1968).

Thus phenomenology opposes reflection to introspection. In order for reflection to be valuable, the experience on which we reflect obviously must not be immediately swept away by the flow of consciousness; it must, then, remain in a certain way identical to itself throughout this process. We see why Husserl sought in *Ideas I* to base the validity of reflection on "retention," a function which must not be confused with memory since it is, on the contrary, the precondition for it: through retention the experience continues to be given to me *itself and in person,* while effecting a different style—that is, in the mode of "no longer." That anger that I had yesterday still exists for me implicitly, since through memory I can recover it, date it, place it, find motivations and excuses for it. It is this same anger which is thus "retained" at the heart of my "living present," since even if I hold—in accordance with experimental laws of memory decay—that the present experience of anger is modified, this implies in reality that in a certain way I still "have" the unmodified anger, in order to be able to "compare" it to the past anger of which my memory presently informs me. The "*Gegenstand*" anger is the same throughout the various evocations that I have of it, since it is always the same anger about which I speak. It is in this way that all reflection proves possible, particularly phenomenological reflection, attempting as it does precisely to restore the experience at hand (the anger) in *describing* it as adequately as possible. This reflection is a descriptive *reprise* of the experience itself, grasped as *Gegenstand* for the present consciousness of the individual describing it. It is, in sum, a faithful rendering of *what* I think of when I think of my past anger. But, again, I must *truly* think this experienced anger, and not some reconstruction of it; I must not allow myself to mask the phenomena really experienced by a prior interpretation of this phenomena.

In this way phenomenological reflection distinguishes itself from the reflection of traditional philosophies, which consisted in reducing the lived experience to its a priori conditions; and thus we find again, at the foundation of this reflection that phenomenology opposes to introspective psychology, the Husserlian concern with the thing itself, the concern with naiveté—that is, the concern which motivates the reduction, the guarantee against the insertion of prejudices and the appearance of alienations in the reflective description I make of anger. It is thus the experience of anger prior to all rationalization, to all thematization, that I must first extract through reflective analysis in order then to reconstitute its meaning.

3. Intentionality and Behavior

Phenomenology—here again in accord with objectivism—was thus necessarily led to reject the classical distinction between interior and exterior. In a sense we could say that the entire Husserlian problem is to specify how there are "objects" for the ego, and this is why it is correct to say that intentionality is at the center of phenomenological thought. Intentionality, taken in a psychological sense, signifies precisely the fundamental inadequacy of any break between interiority and exteriority. To say that consciousness is consciousness of something is to say that there is no noesis without noema, no *cogito* without *cogitatum,* and equally no *amo* without *amatum,* etc.—in brief, that I am interwoven with the world. Recall that the reduction in no way implies an interruption of this interweaving, but only a putting out of play of the alienation whereby I take myself as mundane and nontranscendental. Strictly speaking, the pure ego, if isolated from its contents, is nothing. Thus the psychological ego (which is the same as the pure ego) is always and by its essence thrown into the world, engaged in situations.

We arrive at a new locus of the "psychological" which is no longer interiority, but intentionality—that is, the relation between the subject and the situation, it being understood that this relation does not unite two separable poles, but on the contrary that the ego, like the situation, is definable only in and by this relationship. Against St. Augustine's call for a return to interior truth, Merleau-Ponty writes: "The world is not an object for which I possess within me the law of its constitution, it is the natural milieu and the field of all my thoughts and all my explicit perceptions. Truth does not 'reside' only in the 'inner man', or rather there is no inner man, man is in the world, it is in the world that he knows himself," (*PP*, preface). Thus the world is denied as exteriority and affirmed as "surrounding," the ego is denied as interiority and affirmed as "existing."

Yet this unseating of the central notion of all psychology—namely, the psychological realm itself—occurs in the same way in empirical research. The concept of behavior, as defined by, for example, Watson in 1914, is motivated by the same intention. This behavior is conceived of "peripherally"—that is, it can be studied without appeal to physiology, as a constantly changing relation between a set of stimuli issuing from the natural and cultural environment, and a set of responses to these stimuli performed by the subject in light of his environment. Any hypothesis positing a consciousness enclosed in its interiority and steering this behavior like a pilot steers his craft must be eliminated, for it would be contrary to the only coherent postulate of an objective psychology: determinism. Moreover, such a behaviorist definition permits experimental research and promotes the establishment of constants.

Phenomenology has no need to state its view on this last point, but it could not but applaud the development of an empirical psychology whose principles conformed to the proper eidetic definitions. That phenomenology broke with the reflexology that Watson leaned toward is not surprising, since it viewed this response as a relapse into the paradoxes of introspectionism: instead of remaining at the "peripheral" level, in conformity with his original definitions, Watson was led to seek out the *cause* of the response to a stimulus, in the afferent, central, and efferent nervous transmissions through which the influx is transmitted. Ultimately he even attempted to reduce all such processes to the reflex schema, thus incautiously integrating the results of Pavlov and Bechterev's famous reflexology, and singling out the body once again. The reflex became the foundational concept of behaviorist explanation; yet phenomenologists found no difficulty in showing that Watson is here no longer describing behavior as actually experienced, but a thematized substitute for this behavior, an abstract physiological "model" whose value is questionable.

4. Gestalt Psychology

Before examining how phenomenology uses physiology to criticize Watsonian mechanism, let us first consider Gestalt theory, which of all the psychological schools came closest to phenomenological theses; for the Gestalt psychologists were disciples of Husserl.

The concept of behavior is taken up and clarified by the concept of form (*Gestalt*).[2] Watson's error, as Koffka shows (in *Principles of Gestalt Psychology*), is to have assumed the *objectivity* of behavior. The fact that behavior is observable does not imply that it is an object whose origin must be located in some equally objective connection, like the one that links it to the organization of the nervous system. In reality, the perceptual stimuli which condition our activity, for example, *are not themselves perceived*. If we consider the simple Müller-Lyer phenomenon, where line segments equal in their construction are perceived as unequal, we find a clear case of the difference between what is "objective" and what is "given."

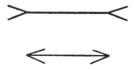

Figure 1

The Watsonian confusion amounts to viewing the given precisely as an "objective" given, since it is the essence of perception to provide us with the objective. But when we assert that this experience provides us with an "illusion," we do not, on the contrary, mean that for any perceiving subject the two segments are actually equal, and that it is only within the frame of reference of the experimenter who constructed the figures that it is an illusion. The mathematical or measurable world in which the figures were constructed is not the perceptual world, and we must distinguish between the perceptual setting and what Koffka called the "geographic" setting—the former being immediately given, the latter constructed through conceptual mediation (for example, the concept of equality, the meter stick, etc.).

The question is not which of these settings is the truer; when

---

2. See P. Guillaume's classic text, *La Psychologie de la Forme* (Flammarion, 1937).

we speak of optical illusions, we unduly privilege the scientific and constructed setting. In fact, *it is not a question of knowing whether we perceive the real as it is* (here, for example, the equality of the two segments), *since the real is precisely what we perceive.* In particular, it is clear that the conceptual and instrumental apparatus of science get their efficacity from the immediate relation of the subject using them to his world; and this is what Husserl had in mind in showing that scientific truth is, in the final analysis, itself founded only on the prepredicative "experience" of the scientific subject. When we ask whether the empirical subject perceives the real itself, we place ourselves in some way above this relationship, and the philosopher thus contemplates the relation between consciousness and object from on high, and with a feigned absolute knowledge. As Plato's *Republic* already made clear, realizing that we are in the cave presupposes our having been outside it. Phenomenology, in relying on the empirical results of Gestalt psychology, denounces this *inversion of order.* We can view the intelligible Platonic world as the set of constructions which form the basis for scientific explanation of the sensible world; but there can be no question of our starting from these constructs—we must, on the contrary, understand the immediate on whose basis science spells out its system. In any case, this system must not be "reified," since it is, as Husserl said, only a "clothing" of the perceptual world.

Consequently, what Koffka called the behavioral surrounding (*Umwelt*) constitutes the actually real universe, since it is actually perceived as real; and Lewin extends this line of thinking in showing that we must rule out any substantialist interpretation of the geographic surrounding, just as with the behavioral surrounding: it is only insofar as these two "universes" are reified that the problem arises concerning their relationship, and particularly concerning their antecedence or even their relative causality. If we hold, on the contrary, that the issue at hand turns only on operative concepts, the problem vanishes. Thus the term "reality" in no way implies a return to a material substance. We would rather define it as a *preexistence.*

An essential character of the phenomenal *Umwelt,* as Koffka also called it, is that it is always *already there.* In a sense the whole of Merleau-Ponty's book on perception consists in drawing out this kernel of *already,* which he sometimes calls the "prehistory"—thus signifying that any objective experimental attempt to derive the manner of my relation to the world invariably returns to an *already* instituted manner prior to all predicative reflection, and precisely upon which the explicit relation that I have with the world is established.

Consider, for example, Wertheimer's experiment:[3] a subject, placed in a room so that he can see it only through a mirror inclined forty-five degrees from vertical, at first sees this room as slanted. Any movement that occurs seems strange to him: a walking man seems to lean, a falling body seems to fall at an angle, etc. After a few minutes, however (if the subject does not attempt to view the room other than through the mirror), the walls, the displaced man, the falling body, all appear "right," vertical, and the impression of tilt disappears; this amounts to an "instantaneous redistribution of up and down." We might say, in objectivist terms, that the vertical had "pivoted"; but any such expression would be erroneous precisely because for the subject this is not what happened. What took place then? The image of the room in the mirror appears to him at first as a strange spectacle, and this strangeness itself guarantees that it be a spectacle, that is, the subject "is not in contact with the utensils that the room contains, he does not live there, he does not cohabit with the man that he sees coming and going." After a few moments this same subject feels able to live in this room, "in place of his true arms and legs he feels the arms and legs he would have to have to be able to walk and act in the reflected room, he lives within the spectacle" (*PP,* 289 [250]).

This signifies, among other things, that the directions up and down, which govern our relation to the world, cannot be defined on the basis of the axis of symmetry of our body, conceived of as a physiological organism and system of objective reactions; and the proof of this is that our body could be shifted *in relation to* up and down, which thus remains *for us* independent of its position. Is this to say that the vertical exists *in itself*? This is no less

---

3. "Experimental Studien über das Sehen von Bewegung," cited by Merleau-Ponty in *PP,* 248 [287].

erroneous, since Wertheimer's experiment, or Stratton's on vision with inversion of the retinal image,[4] show on the contrary that we can speak of objective spatial directions, but not of *absolute* directions; and this impossibility is inevitable insofar as we situate ourselves *within perception,* in the same way that previously we could criticize the perception of inequality of the line segments only by standing outside of perception. But the new spatial direction does not appear as a modification of the old—just as in Stratton's experiment the subject wearing inverting lenses wound up situating himself in an up-down orientation, both visual and tactile, no longer viewed as the inverse of the "ordinary" vertical. On the contrary, the "new" vertical is experienced as vertical plain and simple, that is, precisely as an objective spatial direction.

We find here the very nature of the Gestalt: it is not *in itself*—that is, it does not exist independently of the subject who fits his relation to the world inside it—yet it is neither *constructed by the subject* in the simplistic sense in which Condillac pretended that the rose was constructed through the relation of data from various sensory fields. It is not absolute, since experimentation proves that it can be varied: such is the case in the classic experiments of attention-shifts (for example, with a black Maltese cross inscribed in a circle with a white "field"). It is not purely relative to me, since it gives me an objective *Umwelt.* Associationism never understood how this rose, composed on the cortical level and in an immanent way, could be grasped as it actually is, as transcendent. Thus the *Umwelt* that we place ourselves in through perception is objective, transcendent, but not absolute, since in a sense it is fair to say that we confer this objectivity upon it *already;* but we do so on a level deeper than we realize, on a primordial level that grounds our relation to the world.

We might conclude, then, that Gestalt theory sought to reveal a fundamental *Lebenswelt,* beneath the explicit and limpid universe in which we 'make a living' in the natural and natural-scientific attitudes. Such was the ambition of the later

---

4. Described and commented upon by Merleau-Ponty in *PP,* 282 ff. [244 ff.].

Husserl, and Merleau-Ponty seems to follow the most rigorous line of phenomenological thought when he returns to Gestalt psychological results and interprets them in the manner laid out above. The very tackling of the problem of perception is symptomatic: for it is through perception that we are in the world—or, we might say, that we "have" a world; and it thereby constitutes the core of all philosophical and psychological understanding of humankind. Yet Gestalt theory also focuses primarily upon perception, and Husserl, for his part, returned constantly, as we know, to the problem of the constitution of the *thing*.

This convergence is no coincidence: it stems from the concern with radicality which, moving beneath behavior—itself taken as a relation between a subject and his *Umwelt*—seeks to ground its possibility upon a still more originary relation. It is essential that this originary basis be sought, as much by psychologists as by phenomenologists, not on the side of the physiological organism, but *at the heart of the relation itself*. There can be no question of seeking its explanation in one of the poles of the relation, since this relation itself gives meaning to the two poles it unites. Thus we find again, inherent in the concept of Gestalt, the central notion of phenomenology: intentionality. But this is obviously not the intentionality of a transcendental consciousness; it is rather that of a *"Leben,"* as Husserl said, the intentionality of a subject buried deep within the primordial world, and this is why Merleau-Ponty seeks its source in the body itself.

5. The Problem of the Body

But is this not a return to the physiologism that equates the transcendental subject with the body, leading ultimately down the path Watson followed? No, but it is still true that some Gestalt psychologists felt tempted by physiologism, and avoided it only in settling on the neighboring position of "physicalism." In investigating the relation between the phenomenal and geographical fields, Koffka shows that they are both grounded in the physical world, and that physical science reveals Gestalt phenomena in this world (for example, the distribution of electric current in a conductor).

Yet if we try to interpret the *causes* of psychological Gestalts —that is, to explain *why* it is not the geographical field that is perceived, but the phenomenal—we must refer in the last analysis to physiological Gestalts, where the secret of this "deformation" resides. It is because of the structures to which our nervous system conforms that objects of perception are perceived according to certain constants: the interposition of these constants, or Gestalts, between the world and my ego translates the transformation that my physiological system imposes on physical data. Thus, to the physics of visual information there corresponds a physiology of their transduction, and to this, in turn, a psychology of their translation.

We must therefore assume, as a working hypothesis, an *isomorphism* opening the way to *explanatory* research; the simple comprehensive description of experience must be extended to causal interpretation. There can be no question, of course, of espousing some outdated parallelism here. For we now know, as the physiologist himself admits, that it is impossible to find a "representation" or even a strictly isolated "function" for each cortical site. On the contrary, we know that cortical areas are involved with neural inputs according to certain structures, and that, on the psychological level, what is important is not so much the molecular processes as the global distribution of the input— that is, the relation between areas and the equilibrium or disequilibrium of the input's charge. Neurons do not function as independent units, but as parts of a whole, and it is impossible to explain physiological processes on the basis of their "elements." These regulative structures, which can themselves be understood on the model of physical mechanisms (the field of force, for example), clarify the structures that govern the peripheral level, that is, the psychological. Koffka, and Guillaume after him, thus moved toward a structuralist behaviorism, and it was no accident that the vocabularies of the two schools ended up converging.

Phenomenologists could not find such a convergence satisfying, and it is precisely on this point that their agreement with psychology ends. If we pass from *understanding* structures to *explaining* them, we abandon precisely what is interesting in the concept of Gestalt, namely that in some way it implies an intentionality, and is indissociable from a *meaning*. When Koffka turns to the explanation of psychological structures through neural morphology, he *once again inverts the true psychological problem;* for clearly even the subtlest explanation of the physico-chemical phenomena that "accompany" vision cannot account for the very fact of seeing. If I follow the process in physiology step by step, from the "excitation" of the retina to the visual "center," through the complex of relays and the transmission of the input to the areas permitting accomadation, etc., my schema could be as empirically adequate as I please, but it could never account for the fundamental fact that *I see.* "We have examined a dead eye in the middle of the visual world in order to account for the visibility of this world. Why, then, would it be surprising that consciousness, which is absolute interiority, refuses to be tied to this object?" (Sartre, *BN,* 367 [403–404]). In other words, there is no possible union between the *objective* body studied by the physiologist, and *my* consciousness; on this level any return to physiology, as we already said of Watson, reintroduces the insurmountable contradictions of the classical mind-body problem. If psychology must be in the first person, then it cannot turn to physiology, in the third person, for a solution to its problems.

We must admit, however, that the "absolute interiority" invoked by Sartre in opposing consciousness to the objective body does not strictly follow the phenomenological tradition: interiority leads us to introspection, and we fall back into the somewhat dated dilemma of an untransmissable subjectivity and an objectivism lacking its object. In any case, as concerns this problem—which we take as the key to the phenomenological stand on psychology—the Sartrian position tends to dissociate completely the physiological data from intentional analysis itself. Thus, in *The Psychology of Imagination* (*L'Imaginaire*), Sartre devotes one part to pure eidetic description of imaging consciousness and, admitting that "reflective description does not tell us directly about the representative matter of the mental image," he proceeds in the next part to examine the experimental data; but these latter happen to require a revision of the phenomenological description. Likewise in *Sketch for a Theory of Emotions,* the Gestalt psychologist Dembo's attempts to interpret anger, for example, in terms of environment, phenomenal field of forces, and structural equilibrium are rejected by Sartre because they do not meet up to the requisite intentionality of the constituting consciousness. Finally, in *Being and Nothingness* the lived body is passed over as physiological organism, and considered as experienced facticity, as an object for the Other, but also as that by which "my most intimate inside" is exteriorized under the gaze of the Other: "my body is there not only as the point of view that I take, but also as a point of view on which present points of view are taken that I could never take; it escapes me everywhere" (*BN* 419 [461]). If it escapes *me,* then there is a *me* which is not it.

Thus the dissociation of intentional analysis from physiological data seems to presuppose one even more serious—that of consciousness from body, or rather of subject from object—since these latter dissociations are an open philosophical question, and no longer simply a methodological error. No integration of body to subjectivity or of subjectivity to body is achieved in depth by Sartre, who follows much more the transcendentalist Husserl than the Husserl of the third period. This same Husserl rejected the theses of Gestalt psychology—though they justified themselves in his name—because the objective notion of structure could in no way serve to describe transcendental subjectivity. Clearly the notion of "passive synthesis" is entirely absent from Sartrian philosophy and psychology, which would reproach Husserl for "putting spirit into things," just as Sartre elsewhere imputes this to Marxism.

6. Phenomenology and Physiology

By contrast, the phenomenological psychology of Merleau-Ponty entertains the discussion on the physiological level itself, as can be seen as far back as *The Structure of Behavior.* The very notion of meaning is secondary, and must be based upon a more originary contact with the world: "the difference between the Gestalt of the circle and the meaning 'circle' is that the latter is recognized by an understanding that generates it as the locus of points equidistant from a center, the former by a subject familiar with his world and capable of grasping it as a modulation of this world, as a circular countenance" (*PP,* 491 [429]).

Thus *meaning does not constitute the ultimate psychological object, it is itself constituted,* and the role of perceptual psychology, for example, is to show how the thing, as meaning, is constituted. The thing is clearly a flux of *Abschattungen,* as Husserl said; we must add, however, that this flux is unified in the unity of a perception. But where does this unity come from, the meaning which for me is this thing? From a constituting consciousness? "But when I understand something—a picture, for example—I am not presently enacting synthesis, I come before it with my sensory fields, my perceptual field, and ultimately with a model of all possible being, a universal montage with respect to the world.... The subject must no longer be understood as synthetic activity, but as *ek-stasis,* and all operation of meaning or of *Sinngebung* appears derivative and secondary in relation to this pregnance of meaning in the signs that define the world" (*PP,* 490 [429]). *Phenomenology of Perception* is a fine, serious description of this "universal montage with respect to the world." The method used is very different from Sartre's: it is a point-by-point consideration of the experimental data, particularly the clinical data of neurological and mental pathology. This method is—as its author admits—only an extension of the one Goldstein uses in *Structure de L'Organisme.*

Consider the case of aphasia.[5] It is classically defined as the total or partial absence of a certain linguistic function—the absence of spoken or written language comprehension (verbal deafness or blindness), the absence of speaking or writing ability, where such absence is not the result of any receptor or peripheral motor trouble. Attempts were made to tie these four functions to their respective cortical centers, and to *explain* this psychopathological behavior on the basis of the physiology of the central nervous system. Goldstein shows that these attempts are necessarily in vain, because they uncritically assume the four-fold division of language as a working hypothesis; yet these cate-

---

5. K. Goldstein, "Analyse de L'Aphasie et Essence du Langage," *Journal de Psychologie,* 1933. On the relation of psychopathology to phenomenology, see the works by Binswanger, Jaspers, and Minkowski cited in the bibliography of *Phenomenology of Perception.*

gories (speaking, writing, etc.) are those of everyday speech, and have no intrinsic value. When the physician studies the syndrome from within these categories, he does not allow himself to be guided by the *phenomena themselves,* but rather colors the symptoms with an anatomy prejudiced by and calculated upon the *psychological anatomy* that common sense inserts beneath behavior. He does physiology within a psychological framework, and this latter is never made explicit.

In fact, if we examine the symptoms of aphasia, we find that the aphasic is not aphasic pure and simple. He can correctly name the color red, for example, through the mediation of a strawberry, even though he cannot name the colors in general. In brief, he knows how to use an entire language, which leads from one "idea" to another without mediation or meditation; but when he must speak using mediating categories, the aphasic is truly aphasic. It is not, then, the acoustic complex which is missing in aphasia, but use of the categorial level; we could also define it as the degradation of language and the descent to an automatic level. In the same way, the afflicted individual neither understands nor retains a story, however short; he does not realize that his present situation, and all imaginary situations, are given to him without meaning. Thus Merleau-Ponty, taking up the analyses of Gelb and Goldstein, distinguishes in the end between a *speaking word* and a *spoken word;* the aphasic lacks the productivity of language.

We are not here seeking a definition of language, but the articulation of a new method. To Stein, who insisted that any serious physiology must proceed in objective terms—measurement of chronaxia, etc.—Goldstein responded that such physicochemical investigation is no less *theoretical* than his own psychological approach; in any case, the point is to reconstruct the "dynamics of behavior," so as long as there is reconstruction and not simply coincidence with the behavior in question, all convergent approaches should be used. There is thus no condemnation of causal methods here: we must "follow the causal explanation in its scientific development, in order to clarify its meaning and put it in its rightful place within the whole of truth. This is why there is no *refutation* here, but only an effort to understand the difficulties peculiar to causal thought," (*PP,* 13 [7], n. 1). The attacks against objectivism and the reduction of phenomenology to a "method of subjectivization" that we find, for example, in Jeanson's *La Phénoménologie* are falsified by the guiding spirit of all phenomenology—beginning with Husserl, who strove for the *overcoming* of the subjective-objective dichotomy.

In psychology this overcoming is achieved as method through the descriptive and interpretive recovery of causal data, and as "doctrine" through the concept of the preobjective *Lebenswelt.*[6] Note also the abandonment of the inductive procedures traditionally set forth by the logical empiricists. We will return to this essential point in discussing sociology; but here again the method presaged and employed by Goldstein entirely satisfies the *requirements* of phenomenology.

7. Phenomenology and Psychoanalysis

Phenomenology's relation to psychoanalysis is ambiguous. Sartre, in the section of *Being and Nothingness* where he spells out his existential psychoanalysis (*BN,* 655–63 [725–34]), levels two criticisms against Freudian psychoanalysis: it is *objectivist* and *causalist,* and it uses the incomprehensible notion of *the unconscious.* As *objectivist,* Freud postulates a "nature," the *libido,* at the base of the traumatic event, and thus of the history of all neurosis. As *causalist,* he introduces a mechanical action of the social milieu upon the subject, on whose basis he elaborates a schema of symbols that allows him to draw out the latent meaning of a dream from its manifest meaning—and this independently of the subject (or of the "signifying ensemble," as Sartre puts it). Finally, if the meaning of a neurosis is *unconscious,* how can it be *recognized* when the patient, with the analyst's assistance, understands why he is ill? More radically still, how could something unconscious have meaning, since consciousness is the source of all meaning? In reality, there is a consciousness of deep tendency—"better that these tendencies not

6. The simultaneous use of experimental data and intentional analysis does not, therefore, signify eclecticism, nor simple utility of method.

be distinguished from consciousness," (*BN,* 662 [733]). The psychoanalytic notions of resistance, repression, etc., imply that the id is not really a thing, a nature (*libido*), but the subject himself in his totality. Consciousness distinguishes the tendency to repress from the neutral tendency, and wishing not to be conscious of the former, it is in bad faith: an "art of forming contradictory concepts, i.e. concepts uniting within themselves an idea and its negation," (*BN,* 95 [98]).

If Merleau-Ponty does not take up this last criticism in *Phenomenology of Perception* ("The Body in Its Sexual Being"), it is no accident. Note that the Sartrean description of bad faith involves a *conceptual* consciousness: with Sartre we remain always on the level of a pure transcendental consciousness. Merleau-Ponty, on the contrary, seeks to spell out the passive syntheses from which consciousness draws its meanings. He writes, "existential psychoanalysis must not serve as a pretext for a restauration of spiritualism"; and further, "the idea of a consciousness transparent to itself, and whose existence always implies consciousness that it exists, is not so different from the notion of the unconscious: the same retrospective illusion is involved in both, in loading into me as an explicit object everything that I would learn afterwards," (*PP,* 436 [380–81]).

The dilemma of the "id" versus transparent consciousness is therefore a false dilemma. There is no unconscious, since consciousness is always present with that of which it is conscious; the dream is not the imagery of an "id" which, taking advantage of my sleeping consciousness, works out its own disguised drama. It is the same ego that dreams and that remembers having dreamt. But if I know what I am dreaming, is the dream then a license I grant to my instincts in bad faith? Not at all. When I dream, I place myself within sexuality—"sexuality is the general atmosphere of the dream"—such that the sexual meaning can be "thematized" only through some nonsexual reference to which I link it. The dream symbolism is only symbolism for the waking individual, who, in light of the incoherence of the dream narrative, seeks to view it with a latent meaning; when he dreams, the oniric scene is immediately meaningful—not incoherent, but neither identified as sexual.

To say, with Freud, that the "logic" of the dream obeys the pleasure principle, is to say that, detached from the real, consciousness lives the sexual without situating it, unable to set it at a distance or identify it—in the same way that "for the lover who lives it, love is not a name, not a thing that one can point out, not the same love spoken of in books and newspapers, it is an existential meaning" (*PP*, 437 [381]). What Freud called the unconscious is in fact consciousness unable to grasp itself as specified—I am "circumvented" within a situation, and understand it only insofar as I move out of it, into another situation. In particular, only this transplanting of consciousness enables us to understand the psychoanalytic cure; for it is on the basis of the present situation, and especially upon the relation I experience with the analyst (transference), that I can identify, name, and ultimately deliver myself from the past traumatic experience.

This revision of the notion of the unconscious obviously assumes that we abandon any deterministic conception of behavior, and in particular of sexuality. It is impossible to isolate instincts at the heart of the subject that reside within and empower his conduct like causes. And Freud himself, in generalizing the sexual beyond the genital, knew that it is impossible, for some given behavior, to separate the "sexual" motivations from the "nonsexual." The sexual does not exist in itself; it is a meaning that I give to my life, and "if the sexual history of a person provides the key to his life, this is because the person projects into sexuality his manner of being with regard to the world, that is, with regard to time and to other people" (*PP*, 185 [158]). There is, then, no causation of behavior by the sexual, but an "osmosis" between sexuality and existence, since sexuality is constantly present to human life as an "ambiguous atmosphere" (*PP*, 197 [169]).[7]

---

7. In the preface Merleau-Ponty wrote for Dr. Hesnard's *L'Oeuvre de Freud* (Payot, 1960), we find a new thematization of the "harmony" between psychoanalysis and phenomenology. The guiding idea is that phenomenology is not a "philosophy of [transparent] consciousness," but the continuous and impossible bringing-to-date of an "oniric Being, hidden by definition"; while, for its part, psychoanalysis ceases—thanks to the work of Lacan in particular—to be misunderstood as a psychology of the unconscious: it attmepts to articulate "this *atemporal,* this *indestructible* in us which is, says Freud, the unconscious itself."

VI

Phenomenology and Sociology

1. Explanation

Before considering specifically sociological problems, we already can draw a conclusion essential to the method of the human sciences from the preceding remarks. Experimental science in general seeks to establish constant relations between phenomena. Establishing that such a relation is constant calls for numerous observations and experiments where the related terms appear or could appear; hence the traditional procedures described by Claude Bernard and Mill are legitimated. When the correlation between the two terms exhibits a satisfactory frequency, we conclude that the terms are constantly linked, *ceteris paribus*—that is, as long as certain conditions are met. Research thus constructs a constellation of factors within which the constant can be verified. Philosophy of science thus finds itself led to abandon the category of cause and the corresponding notion of a linear chain; they are replaced by the more supple notion of a set of conditions, and the idea of a network-level determinism. But this development does not change the objective of experimental science, namely explanation.

The law, or constant relation between a set of conditions and an effect, is not in itself explanatory, since it answers only the question how, and not the question why. Theory, elaborating on the infrastructure of a body of laws concerning the same domain of nature, seeks to draw out their common *reason*. Only then is the mind satisfied, for it holds the explanation of all phenomena subsumed by the theory through its laws. The explanatory process thus passes necessarily through an induction; and this latter, if empiricist methodology is to be believed, consists in an inference from observed facts to a constant relation of succession or simultaneity between certain of them. The observation-relative constant is then universalized into an absolute constant, barring possible falsifying observations.

Applied to the human sciences, such a method of research at first glance presents no particular difficulties; we might even say that it offers a guarantee of objectivity. Thus, in proposing to treat social facts *as* objects, Durkheim attempted to spell out an explanatory method in sociology: he aimed explicitly, in *The Rules of Sociological Method,* at establishing constant relations between the "institution" studied and the "internal social milieu" itself defined in terms of physics ("density," "volume," etc.). Durkheim thus proved faithful to the Comtean program of "social physics," and he led sociology toward the predominant use of comparitive statistics. This proceeds by placing a given institution in relation to various sectors of the same social milieu or to various different social milieux, and determining constants for the conditioning of this institution from a detailed study of the correlations established. We could, in generalizing as far as possible, then spell out the laws of the social structure.

Of course Durkheim cannot be reduced to such a static sociology. For he has himself made recourse to genetic or historical explanation—for example, in his study of the family, and in the *Revue de Metaphysique et de Morale* of 1937 he made a clarification of his position, in which he distinguished the problem of genesis of institutions ("what are the causes which bring them about?") from the problem of their function ("what are the ends that they serve, the way they function in society, that is, the ways they are employed by individuals?"). Sociology pursues this double research, using statistics for the latter inquiry and history and comparative ethnology for the former.[1] Nonetheless, the task of sociology remains exclusively explanatory, both longitudinally (genesis) and transversally (milieu). The determinism resides at the network level, but it is still determinism. We found a parallel methodological attitude in psychology, among the objectivists.[2]

---

1. See G. Davy, "L'Explication Sociologique et la Recourse a l'Histoire d'après Comte, Mill, et Durkheim," *Revue de Metaphysique et de Morale,* 1949.
2. See, for example, Guillaume, *Introduction à la Psychologie* (Vrin, 1946).

2. Understanding

Against this view of science Husserl appealed, like rationalists such as Brunschwicg, to the essential inadequacy of induction. In reality the hypothesis of constancy the empiricist claims to *find* through his observations is *constructed* by the mind, on the basis of possibly only a single observation. We cannot induce a law from a large number of "cases"; this is an "idealizing fiction" fabricated by the physicist, which draws its explanatory power not from the number of facts on which it is based, but from the clarity it brings to those facts. Of course this fiction must then be put to the experimental test, but the fact remains that induction and statistical processing cannot alone constitute the entire scientific procedure—it also involves a creative act of the mind.

In *Crisis* Husserl emphasized that Galileo had already established an *eidetic* of the physical object, and that one cannot obtain the law of falling bodies by inducing the universal from various experiences, but only by the "gaze" (*Wesenschau*) constituting the essence of the material body. Every science begins by establishing a network of essences obtained through imaginary variation and confirmed by real variation (that is, experimentation). After opposing it to the induction of the empirical sciences, Husserl ends up making eidetic phenomenology into a moment of natural consciousness. It is thus a caricature of physical methodology, and not this methodology itself, that the objectivists (who are in fact scientists) attempt to impose on the human sciences. We must dissociate a certain logic of science venerated by empiricism and positivism, from scientific practice as actually experienced, which must first be rigorously described.

The Durkheimian attitude, for example, is shot through with Comtean prejudices; for if we wish to study the existence of an institution in a given group, its historical genesis and present function will not alone explain it. A definition of *what* this institution is proves indispensable. For instance, in the *Elementary Forms of Religious Life,* Durkheim assimilates religious life and experience of the sacred; he shows that the sacred itself has its origin in totemism, and that totemism is a sublimation of the social. But does the experience of the sacred itself constitute the essence of the religious life? Could we not conceive (through imaginary variation) of a religion not based on such practice of the sacred? And, finally, what does the sacred itself mean? The constituting of the essence must constantly correct observation, lest the observational results be blind, and stripped of *scientific* value.

The objectivist fixation in the human sciences inevitably bars our knowing the nature of the thing studied. It is, in sum, a prejudice, and it is not by chance that Merleau-Ponty, in his *Cours,* ultimately denounces the existence in Guillaume of "philosophical" presuppositions. We must turn "to the things themselves," describe them correctly, and draw from this description an interpretation of their *meaning;* this is the only true objectivity. To treat humans as things, whether in psychology or sociology, is to assert a priori that the would-be natural method holds equally for physical and human phenomena. Yet we cannot prejudge the issue. If, as Husserl previously called us to do, we seek to describe the procedures of the human sciences, we discover, at the very heart of the inquiry that psychology or sociology brings to the psychological or social, the thesis of an absolutely original modality: the meaning of the behavior studied, whether individual or collective.

This *assumption of meaning* is ususally omitted in a description of methodology, especially objectivist methodology; it amounts to the immediate admission that the behavior *means* something or expresses an intentionality. What distinguishes, for example, the natural object from the cultural object (a pebble from a pen) is that a practical intention is crystallized in the latter, while the former means nothing. Of course a cultural object is a somewhat privileged example, since it is precisely a material configuration *intended explicitly* to satisfy a need: it is the result of work, that is, of the imposition of a premeditated form onto matter. But when faced with prehistoric flints, or a Phonecian altar, we do not immediately penetrate the point of these objects—we puzzle over their purpose; yet in any case we continue to assume that there is a purpose, a meaning to these objects. We realize that there is meaning in human phenomena, even, and perhaps above all if, we fail to understand immediately what this meaning is.

What we said above concerning aphasia implies a thesis of this sort: the point was to show, on the basis of (properly described) observations, that aphasic behavior is indeed behavior—i.e. that it harbors a meaning—and the psychopathological task was thus not simply to establish relations among conditions characterizing the aphasic syndrome, but to draw together the set of these conditions in the unity of aphasic behavior by *understanding* the deep and (if we may so put it) preconscious meaning of this behavior. We never approach a human phenomenon—that is, behavior—without projecting upon it the question, what does it mean? And the true method of the human sciences is not to reduce this behavior, and the meaning it bears, to its conditions—and so dissolve it—but ultimately to answer this question, using the conditioning data clarified by objective methods. To really explain in the human sciences is to understand.

The objectivist pretends that a purely "external" access to individual or collective behavior is not only possible, but desirable. It is only right, he emphasizes, to be on guard against the spontaneous interpretations we project onto the behavior observed. Clearly the immediate understanding that we have of a withdrawn young girl on the sidelines of the dance floor or the playground bears no guarantee of truth. This sort of spontaneous and "evident" understanding results, in reality, from complex sedimentations of our individual history and of the history of our culture; in other words, we must first do a sociology or psychology of the observer in order to understand his understanding.

But this is no reason to dismiss out of hand all understanding, and to side with the Durkheimian claims: this covers over the problem, but it does not resolve it. Between the simplistic subjectivism which amounts to the ruin of all social or psycholgical science, and the brutal objectivism whose laws ultimately lack objects, there remains a place for a *recovery* of explanatory data which seeks to express the unity of their latent meaning. Freud understood this. The kernel of meaning is not hit upon immediately, and this is precisely what phenomenologists emphasize when, in agreement with objectivism, they criticize introspection. But when, for example, Monnerot, in arguing for phenomenology, writes that "understanding is immediate evidence, while explanation is an after-the-fact justification of the presence of one phenomenon by the alleged existence of another phenomenon," he is clearly comparing two incomparable attitudes. For understanding, as evident and immediate grasp of the meaning in, for example, the act by which the butcher tosses his meat on the scale, can hardly serve sociology; it would act rather as the manifest meaning of a dream masked for the analyst, who must decode the latent meaning from it. Sociology cannot make use of such simple understanding, and all of Monnerot's book is an enormous misunderstanding of the word "understanding," as becomes clear when he specifies what this "understanding-sociology" amounts to. Durkheim is struck down (not without naiveté, in fact), but what will replace him? We have already had occasion to note that a certain subjectivism is the infantile disorder of phenomenology. No doubt one can do a sociology of this disorder.

3. The Originary Social: Foundation of Understanding

This methodological detour leads us to the very heart of the sociological problem, at least so far as it concerns phenomenology. Even before being a problem of method, this issue is a problem of ontology: only an adequate eidetic definition of the social permits a fruitful experimental approach. As we noted elsewhere, this does not imply that we must set out a priori a "theory" of the social, nor that the scientific data must be forced to agree with eidetic conclusions. In reality this indispensable eidetic must construct itself in the course of an exploration of the facts themselves, and even afterwards. It is a critique, but as Husserl said, every critique shows its positive side, its positivity.

Yet the understanding under discussion here, at work in all knowledge in the human sciences, expresses my fundamental relation with the Other. In other words, all human science posits the existence of meaning in what it studies. This meaning is not simply a function of utility; it cannot be correctly identified without referring to the person or persons studied. Thus in every human science there is an implicit "postulate" of the comprehensibility of humans by humans; and consequently the relation of the observer to the observed in the human sciences is a case of the relation of person to person, of Me to You. So any human science, and especially sociology, contains within itself an originary sociality, where we understand by this the relation by which subjects are given to one another. This originary sociality, as the ground of all social scientific knowledge, demands an explanation, whose results can then be appropriated in order to clarify social science itself. "The social is already there when we know it or judge it.... Before coming to consciousness, the social exists blindly, and as a call to us" (Merleau-Ponty, *PP*, 415 [362]). Recall the theoretical elaboration of the Other, already outlined in our discussion of Husserl[3]: how is it that I do not perceive the Other as an object, but as an *alter ego*? The classical hypothesis of analogical reasoning presupposes what it is meant to explain, as Husserl's disciple Scheler showed (in *Essence et Forme de la Sympathie*). For a projection of experiences behind the Other's behavior, corresponding to my experiences for the same behavior, implies on the one hand that the Other is seen as *ego,* that is, as a subject inclined to have experiences within himself; and on the other hand that I see myself "from the outside," that is, as an Other for an *alter ego*—since my behavior, to which I assimilate the observed behavior of the Other, can only be lived by me, never apprehended externally.

This, then, is a fundamental condition for the possibility of understanding the Other: that I am not pure transparency for myself. This point was already made concerning the body.[4] If one insists on situating the relation with the Other on the level of transcendental consciousness, it becomes clear that only a game of reciprocal destitution or degradation can be set up between these constituting consciousnesses. The Sartrean analysis of Being-for-Others, proceeding essentially in terms of consciousness, runs up inevitably against what Merleau-Ponty calls "the absurdity of a solipsism for many." "The Other," Sartre writes, "as gaze is nothing but that—my transcendence transcended" (*BN,* 321 [352]). The presence of the Other is made manifest by my shame, my fear, my pride, and my relations with the Other can only be of a negative nature: love, language, masochism, indifference, desire, hatred, sadism. But the correction Merleau-Ponty brings to this interpretation reorients our analysis of the problem of the Other: "In fact the gaze of the Other transforms us into objects only if we withdraw into the base of our thinking nature, if we make ourselves into an inhuman gaze, if each feels

---

3. See above, part 1, "Transcendental Idealism and Its Contradictions."
4. See sect. 5 of the previous chapter.

his actions not taken up and understood but observed like those of an insect" (*PP,* 414 [361]). We must descend beneath the *thought* of the Other and recover the possibility of an originary relation of understanding, without which the feeling of solitude and the concept of solipsism themselves make no sense for us. We must consequently discover, prior to any separation, a coexistence of the ego and the Other in an intersubjective "world," on whose basis the social itself draws its meaning.

This is precisely what we learn from child psychology—itself a sort of sociology. From the sixth month the child's experience of the lived body develops. Wallon notes at the end of his observations that it is impossible to distinguish in the child an interoceptive (coenesthesic) knowledge of his body from a knowledge "from the outside" (for example, in a mirror image); the visual and the interoceptive are indistinct. There is a "transitivism" by which the child identifies himself with the mirror image: the child believes simultaneously that he is where he feels himself and where he sees himself. Even when faced with another's body, the child identifies himself with this Other: the *ego* and the *alter* are not separated. Wallon characterizes this period by the expression "incontinent sociability," and Merleau-Ponty takes up and extends this in the notion of syncretic sociability.[5] This indistinction, this experience of an interworld where there is no egological perspective, is expressed even in language, well after the reduction of the mirror image to an unreal "appearance" has been effected. "The child's first word-phrases deal as much with others' behavior and actions as with his own."[6] The consideration of his own subjectivity as absolutely original perspective comes only later, and at any rate the "I" is used only once the child has realized "that the 'you' can be addressed to himself just as much as to others," and that anyone can say "I" (as Guillaume observed). At the critical age of three Wallon notes a number of traits characteristic of the passing of "transitivism": a desire to do things "by oneself," inhibition when watched by another, egocentrism, duplicity, and transactional attitudes (for example, sharing or stealing toys).

---

5. "The Child's Relation With Others," in *The Primacy of Perception.*
6. Ibid.

Wallon shows, however, that transitivism is still not suppressed; it is prolonged beyond this distancing of the Other, and for this reason Merleau-Ponty opposes Piaget's thesis that at about twelve years of age the child effects the *cogito* and "arrives at the truths of rationalism." "Children must in some way prove to be right, *contra* the adult and Piaget, and the uncivilized mentality of the early years must remain as an indispensible acquisition beneath the adult mindset, if there is to be a unique intersubjective world for the adult" (*PP,* 408 [355]).

In effect Merleau-Ponty claims that love, for example, constitutes an expression of this state of undividedness with the Other, and that, at least in the realm of feeling, transitivism has not been abolished. Note the difference from the Sartrean conclusion: in *Being and Nothingness* Sartre writes that "the essence of relationships between consciousnesses is not *Mitsein,* but conflict" (*BN,* 502 [555]). Yet a phenomenological analysis seems on the contrary to show, on the basis of the human sciences, that the ambiguity in the relation to the Other which we have considered as a theoretical problem gets its meaning from a *genesis* of the Other for me: the meanings of the Other for me are sedimented in a history that is not first of all mine, but a history of many, a transitivity, where my own point of view is only slowly drawn (through conflict, of course) from the originary interworld. If there is a social realm for me, it is because I am originarily of the social; and the meanings that I inevitably project onto the behavior of the Other, when I know that I understand or have understood it, stem from the fact that the Other and I have been and remain comprehended within a unique network of behavior, and in a common flux of intentionalities.[7]

---

7. It seems clear that the inquiry at the level of child psychology, and Merleau-Ponty's appropriation of these results, point in the same direction as the Heideggerian reflection on *Mitsein* which Sartre criticized (cf. *BN,* 303ff. [332 ff.]). But we can still make use of Sartre's criticism, where he qualifies the foundationless assumption of the Heideggerian thesis by adding that "it is precisely this coexistence which must be explained." In the appropriation of experimental data this coexistence is, if not *explained* (which is unthinkable for a human science), at least *explicated,* uncovered, and developed in its originary meaning. We must be sensitive here to the fact that this originarity is at the same time both genetic and ontic.

4. Phenomenology and Sociology

There can be no question, then, of viewing the social as an object. "It is just as false to place ourselves within society as an object among objects, as to put society within us as an object of thought; and both of these errors consist in treating the social as an object" (*PP*, 415 [362]). Monnerot proclaims with great fanfare that "society does not exist." This is true to the extent that it is not a visible reality like an individual—an idea that is not, after all, very new; but it is only one step from there to the reduction of social facts to individual behavior, and the transformation of Durkheimian sociologism into a "social psychology" pure and simple—a step that many modern sociologists take, apparently unaware of its gravity. For the social then becomes simply a personal representation, it is a social for me and according to me, and sociological inquiry bears not on the real modalities of *Mitsein* but on what individuals think of these modalities. We find countless examples of this shift in contemporary sociology; we need consider, for example, only the work of Warner or Centers on social classes.[8] Thus the problems of sociology are dodged. Monnerot's remarks lead in this direction, and we cannot question their theoretical solidity strongly enough. But what sociology, then, does phenomenology propose?

Once again, it does not propose *a* sociology.[9] It rather proposes an appropriation, a critical and constructive reinterpretation of sociological research. There is no phenomenological sociology; there is a philosophy which "speaks, like sociology, only of the world, people, and the mind."[10] Yet this philosophy distinguishes

8. See the fine critical study by A. Touraine: "Classe Sociale et Statut Socio-economique," *Cahiers Internationaux de Sociologie* 11 (1951).

9. We can clearly speak of a "phenomenological school" in sociology: Scheler, Vierkandt, Litt, Schütz, and Geiger would be representatives. (Cf., for instance, Cuvillier, *Manuel de Sociologie* I, pp. 49 ff., pp. 162 ff., and bibliography.) In reality all of the attacks brought against these attempts, more "philosophical" than sociological, are justified in the end. When Mauss insists that general sociology step in only at the end of concrete research, he is in line with contemporary phenomenology, as we will see. In any case of causation, research into *originary* sociality entails only that the definition of sociality come *prior* to the examination of its concrete forms.

10. Merleau-Ponty, "Philosophy and Sociology" in *Signs,* p. 138.

itself from any sociology, because it does not objectivate its object, but aims rather to *understand* it at the level of the transitivism revealed by child psychology. In the case of primitive societies, this operation is no doubt difficult: here intentional analysis does not yield us something like our own world, but a world whose deep structure escapes us. We must, nonetheless, not conclude that they are incomprehensible; and Levi-Bruhl himself, having originally drawn just that conclusion, renounced it in his posthumous *Carnets*. As for Husserl, he wrote to this same Levi-Bruhl in 1935, concerning his *Mythologie Primitive*: "It is a possible task, of much importance, a great task to project ourselves into a humanity closed within its living, traditional sociality, and to understand it insofar as, in its social life and on that basis, this humanity possesses the world which is not for it a representation of the world, but the world that is real for it."[11] In the same way we must appreciate Claude Lefort's angle[12] in the interpretation he gives to the celebrated work of Mauss on *The Gift*,[13] in opposition to the structuralist reading Levi-Strauss gives in his introduction, for Mauss clearly leans much more toward an understanding of the gift than toward a formal systematization of the social or interpersonal tensions inherent to the gift. Lefort's commentary, which attempts to clarify the gift in light of the Hegelian dialectic of consciousness in conflict, follows a phenomenological line of thought. For the phenomenologist, the social is in no way an object; it is grasped as lived experience, and calls, here as in psychology, for an adequate description of this experience in order to reconstitute its meaning. But this description in turn can only be made on the basis of sociological data, themselves resulting from a prior objectivation of the social.

5. Individual and Society: The Ethnological Problem

Our earlier remarks on the originary social as a dimension of existence, which we drew from child psychology, might seem to militate in favor of a degradation of the social within the individ-

---

11. Cited by Merleau-Ponty in "Philosophy and Sociology," p. 135.
12. "L'Echange et la Lutte des Hommes," in *Les Formes de l'Histoire* (Gallimard, 1978).
13. In *Sociologie et Anthropologie* (PUF, 1950).

ual, and certain passages in Merleau-Ponty's *Phenomenology of Perception* might also suggest this. But in reality phenomenology, in attaching itself to concrete sociological and ethnological research, aims on this basis to overcome the traditional antinomy between individual and society. There cannot, of course, be any question of suppressing the specificity of the sociological and psychological sciences: on this issue phenomenology aligns with the position Mauss sets out in his article "Rapport de la Psychologie et de la Sociologie,"[14] which recommends an overlapping of the two disciplines, without rigid boundaries.

Yet here as in psychology, the results of the theoretical elaboration converge upon those of independent research: thus the American culturist school was led *in fact* to abandon the ossified and contradictory categories of individual and society. When Kardiner takes up and extends the research of Cora DuBois on the culture of the Alor islands in light of the category of "basic personality," he sets out both a methodological approach avoiding the inconsistencies of causal and reductive thought, and a theory of a *neutral* infrastructure on which both the psychological and the social are built. This neutral basis meets the demand for an "anonymous existence"—which amounts to anonymous coexistence—imposed by phenomenological reflection on *Mitsein* and the relation between Being-for-Itself and Being-for-Another. Kardiner sets out (by virtue of a psychoanalytic—or even psychologistic—postulate, to which we will return) to describe the entire experience of the child in its cultural milieu, then to establish correlations between this experience and the institutions of this milieu, and finally to show that the latter are a function of the former.

The women of Alor undertake the agrarian labor. Fourteen days after birth, the child is ordinarily abandoned into the hands of whoever finds him (older siblings, distant relatives, neighbors). Fed only irregularly, the child suffers from hunger, and cannot link its alleviation with the image of his mother. His early learning experiences are not directed or even encouraged; on the contrary, those around him ridicule the child, promoting his frustration and discouragement. The system of punishment and

---

14. In *Sociologie et Anthropologie.*

rewards is unstable and unpredictable, preventing any stabilization of behavior. Control over sexuality is nonexistent.

We can sketch out the basic personality on this basis: "feelings of insecurity, lack of self-confidence, distrust of others and incapability of stable affective attachment, inhibition of men by women, absence of an ideal, and inability to see a task through to its end."[15] Correlatively, certain institutions are apparently derived from these familial frustrations: the vagueness and weakness of religion as dogma and as practice is explained by the weakness of the superego. The belief in benevolent spirits is grounded in the childhood experience of abandonment. The neglect of and lack of initiative in artistic technique, or even in construction, bespeaks weakness of personality. The instability of marriage and the frequency of divorce, the masculine anxiety in the face of women, the exclusively feminine initiative in sexual relations, the importance of financial transactions monopolized by men, which often provoke sexual inhibition in these men—all express the hostility the men bear toward women, rooted in their childhood histories, as well as the aggression, anxiety, and defiance which surrounded their development. Kardiner had psychologists unfamiliar with his conclusions perform Rorschach tests on the inhabitants of Alor, and the results pointed in the same direction as his interpretation. Moreover, analysis of life histories equally confirm—if this is really necessary—the correlation established between childhood experience and integration into the culture.

Several times we have used the word "correlation" in linking together the data of individual history and that of collective culture; we must now clarify this as yet ambiguous term. Kardiner uses the word when distinguishing primary from secondary institutions: the former "are those that pose the fundamental and inevitable problems of adaptation. Secondary institutions result from the effect of the primary institutions on the structure of the basic personality."[16] Focusing just on the

---

15. Claude Lefort, "La Méthode de Kardiner," *Cahiers Internationaux de Sociologie* X, p. 118. Note the negative character of each factor: is the basic personality not defined relative to our own culture and in contrast to it? This relativity is inevitable at the level of understanding, since it is the basis of its possibility.

16. Cited by Lefort, ibid., p. 121.

institution of "religion," we find that in Alor, where children are commonly abandoned, the *ego* remains amorphous and proves incapable of forming an image of gods; while in the islands of the Marquesas, where education is loose and negligent, religious development and practice are secondary, while jealousy motivated by maternal indifference is projected into stories where the ogress plays an important role; and in Tanala, the rigorous patriarchal education and the severe control upon sexuality are manifest in a religion where the concept of destiny exercises a powerful constraint. We can see that Kardiner links secondary institutions—religion, for example—to the basic personality, not in a purely mechanistic fashion, but psychoanalytically, using the concepts of projection and motivation. As for the basic personality, its structure is common to all members of a given culture—and it is ultimately the best means of *understanding* this culture.

Clearly ambiguities remain in Kardiner's formulations: it is especially clear—and this already classic criticism is essential—that education is a primary institution only for the child, not for the basic personality in general. Primary and secondary appear to designate a successive temporal order, but this time cannot be that of the culture itself, whose institutional structures we pretend to isolate, but rather the time of the psychological individual. In reality, education in Alor is strictly dependent upon's women's standard of living, which in turn relies—if we understand it properly—on the society as a whole, including its secondary institutions. The basic personality cannot, then, be understood as an *intermediary* between primary and secondary, even if this is considered as an interrelation of motivations and not as linear causality: for no matter how far we go in specifying the complex network of motivations making up a culture, we will never wind up with the basic data constituting the infrastructure responsible for the style of that culture. We can only say, with Lefort, that *it is at the heart of the basic personality that the institutions themselves get their meaning,* and that only an adequate grasp of this personality by the ethnologist allows us to understand the culture it characterizes. This personality is an integrated totality, and if any institution is modified, the entire structure of the basic personality enters into the change. For example, in the Tanala, the passage from dry rice farming to humid rice farming modifies not only the status of property, but the familial structure, sexual practice, etc. These modifications are comprehensible only on the basis of the meaning that the Tanala project on rice farming, and this meaning in turn takes form only on the basis of the source of all meaning: the basic personality. This personality therefore constitutes the "living society" that Husserl saw as the object of sociology—it is that by which humans actually coexist "in" a society, it is, before all institutions, the "culturing culture" (Lefort). Thus the individual does not exist as a specific entity, since he *signifies* the social, as life histories show; but no more is society a coercive entity in itself, since it *symbolizes* through individual history.

Objective research can thus, if "appropriated," return the truth of the social to us, just as it can unmask the truth of the psychological. This truth, these truths, are inexhaustible, since they are those of concrete human beings. Mauss knew this, but he also knew that they are penetrable by the categories of meaning. Culturism remains, for its part, too beholden to the causal categories of psychoanalysis, already corrected by Merleau-Ponty in his discussion of sexuality. The truth of humanity is not reducible, not even to sexuality or society, and this is why every objective approach must be not rejected, but redressed. More than any other discipline, history, the total science, confirms these results.[17]

---

17. In "Ambiguités de l'Anthropologie Culturelle," the introduction to the French edition of Abram Kardiner's *The Individual in His Society* (*L'Individu Dans Sa Société*, Gallimard 1978), Claude Lefort comes out strongly against Kardiner's positivism, as much in the approach taken toward social facts as in the use of Freudian notions.

VII

Phenomenology and History

1. The Historical

From the outset there is an ambiguity in the word "history," which designates both historical reality and historical science. This ambiguity is symptomatic of an existential equivocation— namely that the subject doing historical science is also a historical being. We also see that the question concerning us here— "How is a historical science possible?"—is linked intimately to the question, "How can and how must the historical being transcend its nature as historical being, in order to grasp historical reality as an object of science?" If we call this nature "historicity," a second question arises: is the historicity of the historian compatible with an access to history that conforms to the conditions for science?

We must first inquire into consciousness of history itself; how does the object History come to consciousness? It cannot be in the natural experience of the passing of time; it is not because the subject "finds himself in history" that he is temporal, but rather that "if he can only exist historically, it is because he is temporal in the basis of his being" (Heidegger, *BT,* sect. 72). What do we mean by a history *in* which the subject finds himself, a *historical object in itself?* We borrow from Heidegger the example of a piece of antique furniture as a historical object. The furniture is a historical object not only as possible object of historical science, but in itself. But what is it, in itself, that makes it historical? Is it because it is, in some way, just like it used to be? No, for it has changed: it is worn out, etc. Is it then because it is "old," out of use? But it might not be, while still being antique furniture. What then is *past* in this furniture? It is, Heidegger

answers, the "world" of which it was part. Thus the object sub-
sists still now, and as such is present and cannot but be present;
but as an object belonging to a past world, this present object is
past. Consequently the object is indeed historical in itself, but in
a secondary way. It is historical only because its provenance is
due to humanity, to a subjectivity having been present. But then
what, in turn, signifies for this subjectivity the fact of having
been present?

Here we are turned back from the secondary historical to the
primary—or better, *originary*—historical. If the condition for the
historical nature of the furniture is not in the furniture, but in the
historical nature of the human world where this furniture had its
place, what conditions guarantee us that this historical element is
originary? To say that consciousness is historical is not simply to
say that there is something like time for it, but that *it is time.* Yet
consciousness is always consciousness of something, and an elucidation of consciousness—as much psychological as phenomenological—sums up an infinite series of intentionalities, i.e.
of consciousnesses *of.* In this sense consciousness is a flux of
experiences (*Erlebnisse*), which are all in the present. On the
objective side, this is no guarantee of historical continuity; but on
the side of the subjective pole, what is the condition of possibility
of this unitary flow of experiences? How can we pass from multi-
ple experiences to the ego, when there is nothing in this ego but
these experiences? "While it is interwoven in this peculiar way
with all of its 'experiences', the living ego is nonetheless not
something capable of being considered *for itself* and taken as an
object of study in itself. Abstracted from its 'manner of relating'
(*Beziehungsweisen*) or its 'manner of comporting' (*Verhal-
tungsweisen*)...it has no content to be explicated, and is inde-
scribable in itself and for itself: pure ego and nothing more"
(Husserl, *Ideas,* sect. 80). Our analysis of the problem of historical science thus leads to a further problem: since History cannot
be given to the subject as the object, the subject must be historical in herself—not accidentally, but originarily. How then is the
historicity of the subject compatible with its unity and totality?
This question of the unity within a succession bears equally on
universal history.

Hume's celebrated formula can further clarify this problem:

"The subject is nothing but a series of states which thinks itself." Here again we find the series of *Erlebnisses*. The unity of this series might be given by an act of thought immanent to this series; but as Husserl notes, this act is added to the series as a supplementary *Erlebniss,* which requires a new synthetic grasp of the series—that is, a further experience. Thus we find ourselves faced with a series incompletable from the start, whose unity will always be in question. Yet the unity of the ego is not in question. "We gain nothing by transforming the time of objects into ourselves, if 'in consciousness' we again make the error of defining it as a succession of nows," (Merleau-Ponty, *PP,* 472 [412]). In this way phenomenology seeks to separate itself from Bergsonism. It is clear that the past as noesis is a "now" *and at the same time* a "no longer" as noema, the future a "now" and at the same time a "not yet." We must not say time flows *in* consciousness—it is, on the contrary, consciousness which, on the basis of its now, deploys or constitutes time. We could therefore say that consciousness now intentionalizes what it is conscious of, in the mode of no longer, or the mode of not yet, or finally in the mode of presence.

But this consciousness would then be contemporaneous to all times, if it is from its now that it deploys time: a consciousness constitutive of time would be atemporal. In avoiding the unsatisfactory immanence of consciousness in time, we end up with an immanence of time in consciousness—that is, a transcendence of consciousness with respect to time which leaves the temporality of this consciousness unexplained. In one sense we have not advanced beyond the original problem: consciousness, particularly the historian's consciousness, simultaneously envelops time and is enveloped by time. But in another sense we have elaborated on the problem without prejudicing its solution, being careful to pose it correctly: time, and consequently history, is not graspable in itself, but must be turned back to the consciousness for which there is history. The immanent relation of this consciousness to its history can be understood neither horizontally, as a developing series—since one cannot draw a unity from a multiplicity; nor vertically as transcendental consciousness setting out history—since one cannot obtain a temporal continuity from an atemporal unity.

2. Historicity

Ultimately, then, in what does the temporality of consciousness consist? We return here to "the things themselves," that is, to the consciousness of time. I find myself in the midst of a field of presences (this paper, this table, this morning); this field stretches out in a horizon of retentions (I again take "in hand" the beginning of this morning) and projects into a horizon of protentions (I will bring this morning to a close over a meal). Yet these horizons are moving: this moment which was present, and *consequently was not thematized as such*, begins profiling itself on the horizon of my field of presences. I grasp it as recent past; I am not cut off from it since I recognize it. Then it distances itself still more; I no longer grasp it immediately, in order to take it in hand I must traverse a new depth. Merleau-Ponty (in *PP*, 477 [417]) borrows the schema below from Husserl (*TC*, sect. 10), where the horizontal line represents the series of nows, the oblique lines the profiles of these same nows viewed from a later now, and the vertical lines the successive profiles of the same now.

"Time is not a line, but a network of intentionalities." When I slide from A to B, I keep hold of A throughout A' and beyond. We might say that the problem has only been pushed back a step: since it amounts to explaining the unity of the flux of experiences, we must here establish the vertical unity of A' with A, then of A" with A' and A, etc. The question of the unity of B with A is replaced by that of the unity of A' with A. This is where Merleau-Ponty, following Husserl and Heidegger, establishes a fundamental distinction concerning our problem of the historian's consciousness: in the *purposive* memory and the *voluntary* evocation of a distant past, there is a place for the syntheses of identification which allow me, for example, to connect *this* joy to its time of provenance, that is, to localize it. But this intellectual operation, performed by the historian, itself presupposes a natural and primordial unity by which it is A itself that I reach in A'. It might be said that A is altered in A', and that memory transforms its object—a rather banal proposition in psychology. To which Husserl responds that this scepticism, lying at the base of historicism, undercuts itself as scepticism, since alteration implies *that in some way we know the thing altered*—that is, A itself.[1] Thus there is a *passive synthesis* of A with its perspectival shadings—it being understood that this term does not explain the temporal unity, but allows us at least to pose the problem correctly.

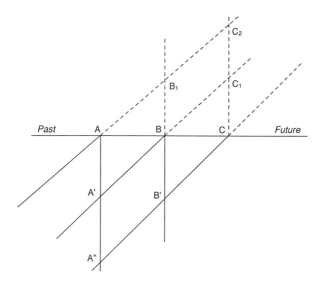

Figure 2

We must still note that when B becomes C, B also becomes B', and that simultaneously A, already fallen into A', falls into A". In other words, my time moves as a whole. What is to come, which I grasp at first only through opaque shadings, comes to pass in person for me; C^2 "descends" into C^1, then gives itself in C within my field of presence, and even as I meditate on this presence C traces itself out for me as "no longer," as my presence is in D. Yet if this totality is given all at once, that implies that *there is no genuine problem of a unification of the series of experiences, after the fact.* Heidegger shows that this way of posing the problem (supposing an *a posteriori* synthesis of a multiplicity of states) characterizes inauthentic existence, which is existence "lost in the They." Human reality (*Dasein*), he says, "does not lose itself in such a way that it must somehow bring itself together from its dis-

---

1. This goes back to the description of reflection and the defense of its worth; see above, chapter 2, sect. 2.

persion afterwards, or in a way such that it must invent a unity which coheres and draws together" (*BT,* sect. 75). And he writes elsewhere that "temporality temporalizes itself as a future which moves into the past in coming to the present" (*BT,* sect. 68d). Thus there is no need to explain the unity of internal time; each now takes up the presence of a "no longer" that it pushes into the past, and anticipates the presence of a "not yet" which will push it in turn. The present is not closed, but transcends itself toward a future and a past; my now is never, as Heidegger notes, an in-sistence, a being contained in the world, but an ex-sistence, or again an ek-stasis, and it is ultimately because I am an open intentionality that I am a temporality.[2]

Before passing to the problem of historical science, a remark on this statement is called for: does it imply that time is subjective, and that there is no objective time? We could answer this question with both a "yes" and a "no." Yes, time is subjective, since time has a meaning, and if it has such it is because we are ourselves time, in the same way that the world has meaning for us because we are world through our bodies, etc.—and this is of course one of the principal lessons of phenomenology. But time is equally objective, since we do not constitute it through an act of thought that would itself be exempt from it; like the world, time is always an *already* for consciousness, and this is why time, no less than the world, is not transparent to us. Just as we must explore the world, we must "travel through" time, i.e., develop our temporality in developing ourselves. We are not subjectivities closed in upon ourselves, whose essence could be specified or specifiable a priori—in brief, monads for whom development would be a monstrous and inexplicable accident—but we rather become what we are and are what we become. We do not have a meaning assignable once and for all, but meaning in process, and this is why our future is relatively indeterminate; why our behavior is relatively unpredictable for the psychologist; why we are free.

---

2. The Husserlian theory of the "living present," as spelled out in unedited manuscripts, is presented in Trân Duc Thao, *Phénoménologie et Matérialisme Dialectique,* pp. 139 ff. See also Jacques Derrida's excellent introduction to his translation of "The Origin of Geometry" (*L'Origine de la Géométrie,* PUF, 1962).

3. The Philosophy of History

We know now how there is history for consciousness: consciousness is itself history. Any serious reflection on historical science must begin with this beginning. Thus, in his *Introduction to the Philosophy of History,* Raymond Aron devotes a chapter to the study of self-consciousness, settling upon the same results: "We have consciousness of our identity through time. We feel ourselves always the same indecipherable and evident being, of which we are eternally the sole observer. But the impressions assuring us of the stability of this feeling are impossible for us to articulate, or even to suggest" (*IPH,* 59 [56]). There is a check upon the objectivist psychologist wishing to specify my history, which is incomplete, that is, unspecifiable. I am not an object, but a project; I am not only what I am, but also what I will be and what I want to have been and to become. But this history which exists for consciousness is not exhausted by the consciousness of its history; history is also "universal history," no longer relative to *Dasein* but to *Mitsein*—it is the history of people.

We do not return here to the question of how there is an *alter ego* for the *ego.* For it is implied, as we have seen, in all of the human sciences. We focus only on the specific way in which the object history presents itself to the historian.

It presents itself through signs, remains, monuments, records, potential material. The furniture that Heidegger discussed returns already, of itself, to the world from which it came. There is a way open to the past, prior to the work of historical science: it is the signs themselves that open this way to us, for we slip immediately from these signs to their meaning. This does not mean that we have explicit knowledge of the meaning of these signs, and that the scientific thematization adds nothing to our understanding, only that this thematization, this construction of the past, is as it were a reconstruction. The signs at the basis of the thematization must already bear in themselves the meaning of a past, or else how could we distinguish the historian's discourse from a fabrication? We return here to the results of the elucidation of meaning. In history we come before a cultural world which must, of course, be reconstructed and reconstituted by a work of reflection (Aron), but this cultural world also comes before us as cultural world: the remains, the monument, the records each return the historian in their own way to a cultural horizon where the collective universe represented there profiles itself, and this grasp of the historical being of signs is possible only because there is a historicity of the historian. "The return to the 'past' is not begun by the appropriation, selection, or guaranteeing of materials; all these already presuppose...the historicity of the historian's existence. This historicity existentially founds history as a science, even for the least noticable dispositions and 'technical apparatus'" (Heidegger, *BT,* sect. 76). And, according to Aron: "All of the following analyses are guided by the assertion that humans are not only in history, but bear within themselves the history they explore" (*IPH,* 11 [10]). Consequently, signs present themselves to the historian immediately invested with a sense of the past; but such meaning is not transparent, and this is why a conceptual elaboration is needed in history. "History belongs not to the order of life, but of the spirit" (Aron, *IPH,* 86 [83]). This means that the historian, on the basis of this procedure, must unveil not laws, or even individual events, but "the possibility which was actually existent in the past" (Heidegger, *BT,* sect. 76). But, Heidegger holds, to achieve this the historian must reconstruct by using concepts. Yet, Aron says, "we always have a choice among numerous systems, since the idea is simultaneously immanent and transcendent to life." We understand this to mean that there is, within a given historical development, certainly a meaning to this development (a "logic," be it economic, spiritual, juridical, etc.), but this meaning or "logic" must be revealed by an act of the historian which amounts to a choice concerning this development. This choice may or may not be explicit, but there is no historical science which does not rely on a philosophy of history. We cannot reproduce here Aron's minute analyses on this subject.

It might be argued that this need for the historian to conceptually elaborate the historical process does not involve a philosophy, but a scientific methodology. No, Aron replies, for historical reality is not essentially constituted as physical reality is, but essentially open and incomplete. There is a coherent physical discourse because there is a coherent physical universe for the physicist; but while the historical universe may well be coherent, such coherence is always unspecifiable for the historian since this universe is not closed. Of course Waterloo is past, and the history of the First Empire is complete; but if we approach this moment of historical becoming as such, we fail precisely to capture it, since for the actors whose world we are trying to restore (the "possibility which was actually existent in the past") this moment presented itself against an equivocal horizon of contingent possibilities. After the fact we declare the fall of the Empire necessary, but this is to admit that we are doing the history of this History from the observer's standpoint, since we say "after the fact," therefore, the history we do is not transcendental science. What is it then? "Historical science is a form of consciousness that a community has of itself" (Aron, *IPH,* 88 [85]), inseparable as such from the historical situation at whose heart it is elaborated, and from the will to know itself. The interpretations given for a single moment of development vary as a function of the moment of development from which they are given. The Middle Ages were not the same for the seventeenth and nineteenth centuries. But is it not possible to envisage, as a primary postulate of the historian's effort, an interpretation adequate to the reality being interpreted? No, Aron again replies, for either this definitive model would proceed along the causal model of the natural science (simplisitic economism, for example), and any such interpretation would fail to grasp the totality of the historical reality, to apply to a total becoming, the final resolution of a free process which outstrips any such "factor"; or else it would be modeled on "understanding," the appropriation of the past through the capturing of its meaning—but precisely this meaning is not given to us in an immediately transparent way. Both causality and understanding have their limits. To overcome these limits we must project a hypothesis concerning this total becoming, which not only recovers the past but grasps the historian's present as past, i.e. as the profile of a future; we must, that is, do a philosophy of history. But the use made of this philosophy is conditioned by a history of philosophy, which in turn manifests the immanence in time of the thinking which desires to be atemporal. Thus Marxism, for example, appears not to be a science but an ideology, not objective knowledge but a political hypothesis about the future. Do we then fall into historicism, resigned to a development without meaning which leads to scepticism, fatalism, and indifference? Not at all, since historicism is itself historically linked to positivism, and its negative theses cannot, any more than the others, be given as absolutely true. Like all scepticism, it negates itself.

4. Historical Science and Historicity

We can see what direction Aron is taking. He is a fair representative of what we might call the right wing of phenomenology, and while his work has no common ground with the text by Monnerot cited above, he submits history to a reduction comparable, in the intellectualism that inspires it, to what Monnerot's work inflicts upon sociology. It is clear that a mechanistic interpretation of history must be rejected; but it is no less clear that a method of understanding fails necessarily to extend into a philosophical *system.*

Certainly the absence of the people who lived the *Mitsein* that the historian studies makes his task even more complex than that of the ethnologist, but the fact remains that this synchronism, as a historical "epoch," harbors a meaning to be understood, without which it would not *be* human history. This meaning must speak to us in some way, from this epoch to our own and ourselves there must be an originary communication, a complicity, and this guarantees in principle the possibility of understanding this past. Ultimately Aron, following Dilthey, emphasizes the discontinuity of historical development, so much so that from one period to another the passage of understanding is blocked, and the historian forced to employ a set of concepts that he projects upon the past blindly, awaiting a reaction like an empirical chemist. But such discontinuity does not exist, since there is a history, that is, precisely an incessant recovery of one's past and a protention toward the future. To deny historical continuity is to deny the meaning within the historical development, yet there must be meaning in this development—not because people think this meaning, or construct systems of the meaning of history, but because in living, and in living together, people exude meaning.

This meaning is ambiguous precisely because it is in the process of becoming. Just as we cannot assign some definitive meaning to a subjectivity, since this subjectivity is cast forward toward a future whose open possibilities will define it further, so the full meaning (the direction) of a historical situation is not assignable once and for all—since the society being affected cannot be viewed as an object evolving according to mechanical laws, and one stage of this complex system is not succeeded by another, but by an array of possibilities. These possibilities are not innumerable, and this is why there is meaning in history, but they are numerous, and this is why the meaning cannot be read off effortlessly. Ultimately this open future, as open, belongs to the present situation itself. It is not superadded, it is extended within it by its very essence. A general strike is not only what it is, but also and not least what it will become. If it ends in setback and frustration for the working class, it will be understood as a repressed outburst, as a rear-guard conflict, or as a warning, according to the stages that follow; or if it is transformed into a political strike, it takes on an explicitly revolutionary sense. In any case, its definitive meaning is approached step by step in the course of historical development, and this is why there is not, strictly speaking, any definitive meaning, since this development is never completed.

Aron's mistake comes in situating the meaning of history on the level of the thinking of this meaning, and not on the level of this meaning as experienced—a mistake sociology revealed to us already.[3] Also, are the difficulties encountered by the historian in restoring the meaningful core of a period—that "culturing culture" on whose basis the "logic" of human development shows through the events and organizes them in a movement—not the very difficulties of the ethnologist? Of course, insofar as the historian studies "historical" societies, he must also uncover the *reason* within the movement, reveal the evolution of a culture, and draw together the possibilities open to each of its stages. Just

3. We find the same attitude in *L'Opium des Intellectuels* (Calmann-Levy, 1955), where Aron, in discussing the meaning of history, makes this statement: "History has, in the final analysis, the meaning that our philosophy attributes to it" (p. 171).

as such understanding involved "an imaginary transposition to understand how the primitive society closes off its future, develops without being conscious of change, and, in some way, constitutes itself in terms of its stagnation," so here it involves "situating oneself in the course of the progressive society in order to understand the movement of meaning, the plurality of possibilities, the still-open debate" (Lefort).[4]

It does not follow, then, that because the historian is himself within history and his thinking is itself an event, the history he constructs is invalid, nor that this thinking cannot be true and must resign itself to simply expressing a transitory *Weltanschauung.* When Husserl argued against the historicist doctrine and demanded that philosophy be a *rigorous science,* he was not seeking to establish a truth outside of history. On the contrary, history remained at the center of his concept of truth[5]: this truth is not an atemporal and transcendent object, but is experienced in the flux of becoming and will be corrected indefinitely by other experiences. It is thus "omnitemporal," on the way to realization, and we can say of it what Hegel said: it is a result— with the qualification that ours is a history without end. The historicity of the historian and his enmeshing in a social coexistence do not bar the doing of historical science—*they are, on the contrary, the conditions of its possibility.* And when Aron concludes that "the possibility of a philosophy of history ultimately merges with the possibility of a philosophy in spite of history" (*IPH,* 320–21 [318]), he implicitly admits to a dogmatic notion of atemporal and immutable truth. This lies at the heart of his thought, involving an entire latent philosophical system, and proves radically contradictory to the view of truth-in-movement that the later Husserl expressed so forcefully.

Thus phenomenology does not propose a philosophy of history, but it responds in the affirmative to the question that began this chapter—at least if the meaning of the word "science" is not limited to mechanism, and if note is taken of the methodological revision outlined in our discussion of sociology.

---

4. Claude Lefort, *Les Temps Modernes* (February 1951).
5. See above, part 1, "The Lifeworld."

It proposes rather a reflective recovery of the data of historical science, an intentional analysis of the culture and period laid out by this science, and the reconstruction of the concrete, historical Lifeworld, through which the meaning of this culture and period is revealed. This meaning cannot in any sense be taken for granted, and history cannot be read through any single "factor," be it political, economic, or racial. The meaning is latent because originary, and it must be resuscitated without being presupposed if we are to be led by "the things themselves." This possibility of recovering the meaning of a culture and its development is grounded in principle upon the historicity of the historian. The fact that phenomenology is itself situated in history, and is viewed by Husserl as an opportunity to safeguard the reason which is essential to humanity,[6] that it attempts to impose itself not only through a pure logical meditation, but through a reflection on current history—all this shows that it does not take itself as a philosophy outside of time, or an absolute knowledge resolving a finite history. It presents itself as a moment in the development of a culture, and does not takes its truth to be contradicted by its *historicity,* since it makes of this very historicity an open doorway to the truth.

This historical meaning that phenomenology attributes to itself is precisely what Marxism contests in assigning it another, quite different meaning.

5. Phenomenology and Marxism

A. The Third Way

It is only fitting to begin by emphasizing the *insurmountable* oppositions that separate phenomenology and Marxism. Marxism is a materialism: it holds that matter constitutes all of reality, and that consciousness is a particular material mode. This materialism is dialectical. Matter develops itself according to a movement whose motive force is the negation, preservation, and sur-

---

6. See above, part 1, "Transcendental Idealism and Its Contradictions."

passing of the previous stage by the following stage—and consciousness is one of these stages. From our present perspective, this signifies in particular that every form of *matter* contains in itself a *meaning,* and this meaning exists independently of any "transcendental" consciousness. Hegel understood the presence of this meaning in holding that the real is the rational, but he imputed it to a fictitious Spirit of which nature and history were only manifestations. Marxism, on the contrary, refuses to separate Being from meaning, as any idealism does.

Certainly the phenomenology of the third Husserlian period seems for its part to refuse such a separation—for example, when Merleau-Ponty, its most remarkable representative, speaks of "this pregnance of meaning in the signs which could define the world." But the whole problem is to specify which "world" this involves. We must take care to note here that the world with which the Husserlian meditation on truth is ultimately concerned cannot be confused with the "material" world. It is rather defined, as we have defined it, on the basis of consciousness, or at least the constituting subject. Husserl claimed that the constitution of the world, as it occurs in the development of subjectivity, is based upon the Lifeworld (*Lebenswelt*), on an originary world which this subjectivity "relates" to by way of passive syntheses. An outline of an empiricism, Jean Wahl concludes.[7] But we do not concur, since it involves a *reduced* subjectivity, and a world no longer the world of natural reality; and Husserl would hardly fall into the errors of empiricism which he so often renounced. As Thao has rightly argued, "the natural reality discovered in the depths of experience is no longer that presented to consciousness spontaneously before the reduction."[8] The reality at issue here is what, following Merleau-Ponty, we have called "existence," "originary world," etc.; and with phenomenology we have always taken great care to guard it against any possible objectivist reading. This reality is not objective, then, but neither is it subjective—it is neutral, or ambiguous. The reality of the

---

7. Jean Wahl, "Notes Sur Quelques Aspects Empiristes de la Pensée de Husserl" *Rev. Méta. Morale* (1952).

8. Trân Duc Thao, *Phénoménologie et Matérialisme Dialectique,* p. 225.

natural world prior to the reduction—that is, ultimately, *matter*—
is in itself stripped of meaning for phenomenology (cf. Sartre).
The different regions of being are dissociated, as Thao also
notes, and, for example, "matter worked over by humans is no
longer matter, but 'cultural object'."[9] This matter gets its meaning only from the categories that frame it as physical reality, such
that ultimately being and meaning find themselves separated by
reason of the correlative separation of the different regions of
being. Meaning is traced back solely to a constituting subjectivity, but this subjectivity is in turn traced back to a neutral world
which is still becoming, and in which the entire meaning of reality is constituted in its genesis (*Sinngenesis*). Consequently, Thao
concludes, the contradiction within phenomenology appears
intolerable. For it is clear that this neutral world holding the sedimented meaning of all reality cannot be other than nature itself,
or rather matter in its dialectical movement. In one sense it
remains true that the world before the reduction is not the same
one found after the analysis of constituting subjectivity: the former is, in effect, a mystified universe where humans are alienated, and precisely this is not reality. Reality is this universe redis-
covered at the end of the phenomenological description, and in
which the truth of experience takes root. But "experience is only
an abstract aspect of *actually real life*"; phenomenology cannot
come to grasp in it the "material content of this life." In order to
preserve and surpass the results of transcendental realism, it
must be extended by dialectical materialism, which rescues it
from its ultimate temptation: backsliding into the "total scepticism" which Thao sees in Husserl's last writings and which seems
inevitable to him if we do not give subjectivity "its predicates of
reality."

We cannot further discuss Thao's remarkable text here; in
any case it sets out clearly the irreducibility of the two theses,
since it is only at the price of identifying originary subjectivity
with *matter* that Marxism can preserve phenomenology in surpassing it. In Lukács's *Existentialisme et Marxisme*[10] we find a

---

9. Ibid., pp. 225–26.
10. Georg Lukács, *Existentialisme et Marxisme* (Nagel, 1948).

quite different Marxist critique, in that it attacks phenomenology not by taking up its thought from the inside, but in studying it explicitly as "behavior." In a certain sense it completes the preceding criticism, since it seeks to show that phenomenology, far from being degraded by its historical meaning, on the contrary finds its truth in it. (We note, incidentally, that Lukács attacks more the Husserl of the second period.)

Husserl had, like Lenin, fought against Mach's psychologism and all the forms of sceptical relativism expressed in Western thought from the end of the nineteenth century. This phenomenological position is explained, according to Lukács, by the need to eliminate objective idealism, whose resistence to scientific progress had finally been vanquished, especially as concerns the notion of evolution. Subjective idealism, on the other hand, led clearly, for an honest thinker like Husserl, to dangerously obscurantist conclusions. Yet materialism still remained unacceptable in Husserl's eyes: subjectively, because he situated himself in the Cartesian line, and objectively in light of the ideology of his class. From there led the attempt, characteristic of phenomenological behavior, to "invest the categories of subjective idealism with a pseudo-objectivity.... (Husserl's) illusion consists precisely in believing that it suffices to turn one's back on all purely psychological methods in order to escape the domain of consciousness."[11] In the same way, if Husserl battled against Mach and the formalists, it was in order to introduce the concept of "intuition" meant to resist relativism and reaffirm the validity of philosophy against the inevitable decline set off by pragmatism. But these themes are "just as much symptoms of the crisis of philosophy." What crisis is this? It is intimately linked to the first great crisis of capitalism, which struck in 1914. Before this philosophy had been put out of play, and replaced by the specialized sciences in the examination of the problem of knowledge: this is precisely the stage of positivism, pragmatism, and formalism, characterized by the confidence of intellectuals in an apparently eternal social system. But when the guarantees accorded by this system since its political birth (liberties of the citizen and respect

---

11. Ibid., pp. 260–62.

for the human individual) began to be threatened by the conse-
quences of that very system, the symptoms of the crisis of philosophical thought became observable: such is the historical context
of phenomenology, taken as behavior. Its ahistoricism, its intu-
itionism, its will to radicality, its phenomenalism, are all ideological factors meant to mask the true meaning of the crisis, to avoid
drawing the ineluctable conclusions. The "third way," neither ide-
alist nor materialist (neither "objectivist" nor "psychologist," as
Husserl put it), is the reflection of this equivocal situation. The
"philosophy of ambiguity" expresses in its own way an ambiguity
of philosophy in this stage of bourgeoise history; and this is why
intellectuals accord it a sense of truth, because it lives this ambiguity, and because this philosophy, in masking its true meaning,
fills its ideological function.

B. The Meaning of History

It is clear, therefore, that no serious reconciliation between
these two philosophies can be attempted, and it bears emphasizing that the Marxists never wanted one; but if they refused it,
this is because they were offered. We are not concerned here
with retracing the history of this discussion. No doubt the political and social experience of the Resistance and the Liberation
are essential factors here, and an analysis of the situation of the
intelligentsia during this period would be called for. Phenomenology has always been led to pit its theses against those of
Marxism; it came to rest spontaneously after the decentering of
the transcendental ego, in favor of the Lifeworld.

Phenomenology contributes essentially to Marxism concerning two theses: the meaning of history, and class consciousness.
In fact, these two theses are the same, since for Marxism the
meaning of history can only be read through the stages of class
conflict, and these stages are dialectically linked to the consciousness that classes have of themselves in the total historical
process. Class is defined in the final analysis by the situation
within the objective relations of production (the infrastructure),
but the fluctuations in its volume and combativeness, reflecting
the incessant modifications of this infrastructure, are in turn
dialectically linked to superstructural factors (politics, religion,
jurisprudence, and ideology proper). For the dialectic of class

conflict—the driving force of history—to be possible, the super-structures must fall into contradiction with the infrastructure or production of material life, and consequently these superstructures enjoy, as Thao notes,[12] an "autonomy" with respect to this production and do not simply evolve automatically in the wake of its evolution. "The autonomy of the superstructures is just as essential to the understanding of history as the movement of productive forces."[13] We thus arrive at the view, taken up by Merleau-Ponty,[14] according to which ideology (in the general sense of the term) is not illusion, appearance, or error, but reality just like the infrastructure itself. Thao writes, "the primacy of economics does not negate the truth of the superstructures, but returns it to its authentic origin, in experienced existence. Ideological constructions are relative to the mode of production, not because they reflect it—which is absurd—but simply because they draw all their meaning from a corresponding experience where 'spiritual' values are not represented, but lived and felt."[15] Thao grants phenomenology the merit of having "legitimated the value of all the meanings of human existence"—in sum, with having helped philosophy to reveal the autonomy of the super-structures. "In attempting to understand the value of 'ideal' objects in a spirit of absolute submission to the *given,* phenomenology succeeds in relating them to their temporal roots without thereby depreciating them."[16] Thao shows that the relation to economics permits a grounding of the meaning and truth of "ideologies"—phenomenology, for example. It allows us, in short, to understand how, and above all why, the bourgeoisie

---

12. Trân Duc Thao, "Marxisme et Phénoménologie," *Revue Internationale* 2, pp. 176–78. This article, which appeared considerably earlier than the book cited above, is more reserved from the Marxist point of view than the theses of the book. We find here an explicit intention to *revise* Marxism. See also P. Naville's response in *Les Conditions de la Liberté* (Sagittaire).

13. Trân Duc Thao, "Marxisme et Phénoménologie," p. 169.

14. Maurice Merleau-Ponty, "Marxisme et Philosophie" in *Sens et Non-Sens,* pp. 235 ff.[English translation: "Marxism and Philosophy" in *Sense and Non-Sense,* pp. 133 ff.].

15. Trân Duc Thao, "Marxisme et Phénoménologie."

16. Ibid., p. 173.

effort in the sixteenth century to escape papal power, for example, took the ideological form of the Reformation; to hold that this form is nothing but an *illusory* (i.e., ideological) reflection of material interests is to refuse to understand history. Thao proposes to explain the movement of the Reformation as the "rationalized" expression of the *actually lived experience* of the new conditions of life brought about by these very bourgeoisie—conditions characterized above all by a security that no longer found it necessary, as the insecurity of the previous centuries had, to close up spirituality in cloisters, but rather permitted the adoration of *God in the world*. There is thus room at the heart of Marxist analyses for phenomenological analyses bearing on consciousness, and allowing us precisely to interpret the dialectical relation of this consciousness, taken as source of the superstructures, to the economic infrastructure where it finds itself engaged in the final analysis (but *only* in the final analysis).

We see the legitimacy, then, in the possibility of a dialectical development of history, whose meaning is at the same time both objective and subjective, that is, both necessary and contingent: humans are not directly rooted in the economic, but in the existential—or rather, the economic *already* belongs to the existential—and they experience their freedom as real. The revolutionary problem, according to Thao, thus lies not simply in organizing and establishing a new economy, but in humanity's realization of the very meaning of its becoming. It is in this sense, according to him, that Marx's theory is not a dogma, but a guide for action.

Merleau-Ponty approaches the same problem, but through its concretely political aspect.[17] To refuse history a meaning is equally to refuse it its truth and its responsibility to the political, to hold that the Resistance worker is no more justified in killing than the collaborater—to claim that "the end justifies the means," as the popular formula would have it. For then the path to an end, set up arbitrarily by a subjective and uncheckable pro-

---

17. See especially *Humanism and Terror,* and two passages from *Phenomenology of Perception*: his note on historical materialism (*PP,* 199–202 [171–73]), and his observations on freedom and history (*PP,* 505–513 [442–450]).

ject, can pass through any route whatsoever—human happiness and freedom could be achieved through Nazism and Auschwitz. History shows that this is not so. We must not only claim that violence is ineluctable because the future is open and "being realized," we must also hold that certain types of violence are more *justified* than others; we must not only agree that the politician never fails to be a Machiavelli, but show as well that history has its ruses, and Machiavellizes the Machiavellis. If history shows, if history works its ruses, it is because it aims at something objective and means something. Here we mean not history itself (which is only an abstraction), but "an average, statistical meaning" of the projects of individuals engaged in a situation, which is specified only by these projects and their results. The meaning of such a situation is the meaning individuals give themselves and others, in a slice of time called "the present." The meaning of a historical situation is a matter of coexistence or *Mitsein;* there is history because people exist together—not as closed, molecular subjectivities added together, but as beings projected toward the Other as toward the medium of their own truth. Thus there is a meaning to history which is the meaning humans give their history *in living.* It becomes clear, then, how different comings-to-consciousness can graft themselves onto an objective base—what Sartre called the possibility of a "breaking free": "an objective position in the process of production never suffices to provoke the coming to class-consciousness" (*PP,* 505 [443]). We do not pass automatically from infrastructure to superstructure, and there is always an equivocation from one to the other.

But if it is true that humans give their history its meaning, where do they get this meaning from? Do they assign it by some transcendental choice? And when we impute the *Sinngebung* to humans themselves, to their freedom, do we not once again "turn history on its head," and return to idealism? Is there an ideological possibility of escaping the dilemma between "objective thought" and idealism? *Economism* cannot explain history, cannot explain how an economic situation "expresses" itself in racism, scepticism, or Social Democracy; nor can it explain how various different political positions can correlate with the same position in the process of production being described, nor how "treason" could arise, nor even why political agitation would prove necessary. In this sense, history is certainly contingent. But neither can *idealism* explain history: it cannot explain why the "Enlightenment" took place in the eighteenth century, nor why the ancient Greeks did not develop experimental science, nor why fascism threatens our own times.

In order to understand history (and there is no greater task for philosophy) we must therefore escape this impasse of equally total freedom and necessity. "The glory of the Resistance, like the shamefulness of the collaboraters, presupposes both the contingency of history—without which there would be no political culpability—and the rationality of history—without which all would be folly" (Merleau-Ponty).[18] "We give history its meaning, but not without it proposing it to us" (*PP,* 513 [450]). This implies not that history has *a* meaning—unique, necessary, and thus inevitable, of which humans are the toys and dupes, as they ultimately are in Hegelian philosophy of history—but that history has *some* meaning. This collective meaning is the result of the meanings projected by historical subjectivities at the heart of their coexistence, and which these subjectivities must recover in an act of appropriation that puts an end to the alienation or objectification of this meaning and history, constituting *in itself* a modification of this meaning and proclaiming a transformation of history. There is not *objectivity* on one side and *subjectivity* on the other, which are heterogenous and at best brought into alignment; and thus there is never a total understanding of history, since even when this understanding is as "adequate" as possible, it engages history in a new way and opens up a new future. For this reason we can grasp history neither through objectivism nor subjectivism, and even less through a problematic union of the two, but only through a deepening of both which leads us to the very existence of historical subjects in their "world," on the basis of which objectivism and subjectivism appear as two equally inadequate options through which these subjects can understand themselves in history. This existential understanding is not itself

---

18. Maurice Merleau-Ponty, *Humanisme et Terreur,* p. 44 [English translation: *Humanism and Terror,* p. 41].

adequate, since people always have a future, and create their future in creating themselves. Because history is never completed—that is, because it is human—it is not a specifiable object; but precisely because it is human, history is not meaningless. Thus we find new justification for the Husserlian motif of a philosophy which is never finished with the question of a "radical beginning."[19]

---

19. We see this again in *Les Aventures de la Dialectique* [English translation: *Adventures of the Dialectic*]: "Today as one hundred years ago, and as thirty-eight years ago, it remains true that no one is a subject or free, that freedoms conflict with and demand one another, that history is the history of their discussion, that it inscribes itself and is visible in institutions, civilizations, and the wake of the great historical actions, that there are means of understanding them and situating them, if not in a system according to an exact and definitive hierarchy, and in the perspective of a *true,* homogeneous, and ultimate society, at least as different episodes of a single life, of which each is an experience and can pass on to those that follow" (pp. 300–301 [pp. 205–206]). But here Marxism is attacked in its fundamental thesis, namely the very possibility of socialism, the classless society, the elimination of the proletariat as a class by the empowered proletariat, and the end of the State: "This is the very question: is revolution a limit case of government or the end of government?"(p. 316 [p. 216]). To which Merleau-Ponty replies: "It is conceived of in the second sense, and practiced in the first.... Revolutions are true as movements and false as regimes" (pp. 316 and 303 [pp. 216 and 207]). We cannot undertake here a critical description of this book; we note only that it exhibits the incompatibility of phenomenological theses with the Marxist conception of history. In particular, Merleau-Ponty's rejection of the genuine possibility of a realization of socialism should not surprise us if we realize that, in refusing any reference to the *objectivity* of the relations of production and their modifications, phenomenologists were led imperceptibly to treat history and class conflict as the development and the contradiction of individual *consciousnesses.*

Conclusion

I.

Phenomenology's discussion of its own historical meaning can be pursued indefinitely, since this meaning is not fixable once and for all. In posing an ambiguous history, phenomenology imposes its own ambiguity on history. Marxism shows, on the contrary, that the supposed ambiguity of history in fact manifests the ambiguity of phenomenology. Unable to cast its lot in with the materialism of the proletariat revolution, it wishes to open a *third way,* and play the bourgeoisie's game objectively—even if, subjectively, the honesty of some of its thinkers is beyond suspicion. It is not by chance that its right wing leans toward fascism, and that its "left" laughably contradicts itself.[1] The philosophy of history hastily constructed by Husserl in *Crisis* cannot be preserved.

II.

It can, however, serve to reveal a truth of phenomenology. For it is clear that this ambiguity in phenomenological theses in turn expresses the intention to overcome the dichotomy of subjectivism and objectivism. This intention is "realized" successively within Husserl's philosophy in the notions of *essence, transcen-*

---

1. Concerning Heidegger, see Thévenaz, *De Husserl à Merleau-Ponty* (Neuchâtel, 1966); and J. M. Palmier, *Les Ecrits Politiques de Heidegger* (L'Herne, 1968). See also the following articles by Sartre: "Matérialisme et Révolution," (written in 1946), in *Situations III*; "Les Communistes et La Paix," *Temps Modernes* (July–October 1952). Equally rewarding reading is offered in the "Réponse à Lefort," as well as the target article, in *Temps Moderne* (April 1953); Chaulieu's response to Sartre in *Socialisme ou Barbarie* 12 (August–September 1953); and Lefort's response, *Temps Modernes* (July 1954).

dental ego, and *Leben.* These concepts have one thing in common: they are all "neutral"; they all seek to establish the "ground" that nourishes the meaning of life. In the human sciences we have seen them spelled out successively in body, *Mitsein,* and historicity. These concepts are aimed not at *system-building,* but at restoring anew the infrastructures of all thought, including systematic thought. But the question is whether the infrastructures, the "things themselves," are discernible *originarily,* independently of all historical sedimentation. By "originarity" we do not mean some hypothetical "in-itself" beyond the intentional aiming: phenomenology begins with the phenomena. But "the phenomenality of the phenomena is never itself a phenomenal datum," as Eugen Fink rightly notes.[2]

Is there not, in sum, a phenomenological decision to assume a viewpoint where "the appearing of the being is not itself a thing that appears"?[3] And phenomenology proves incapable of accounting phenomenologically for this decision to identify being and phenomena. We must, according to Wahl, therefore "establish the right to do phenomenology."[4] But to establish this right is to return to traditional *speculative thought,* to philosophical systematization. To justify intentional analysis is to leave it and make recourse to a system. Fink goes further than Wahl: he shows that, for better or for worse, this recourse is implicit in Husserl's thought: "the construal of the 'thing itself' as phenomenon, the postulate of a radical new beginning, the thesis of the posteriority of the concept, the faith in 'method', the indeterminacy of what counts as 'constitution', the vague character of the concept of *Leben,* and above all the analytical process itself, and more precisely the assertion of the priority of originary modes"—all these belie the speculative elements inherited from modern philosophy, and in particular from the Cartesian revolution of the *cogito.* The *Crisis,* in explicitly situating phenomenology within this heritage, thus constitutes an admission, and we

2. Eugen Fink, "L'Analyse Intentionelle et Le Problème de La Pensée Spéculative," in *Problèmes Actuels de La Phénoménologie* (Desclée, 1952), p. 71.

3. Ibid.

4. Jean Wahl, "Conclusion" to *Problèmes Actuels de La Phénoménologie.*

are not surprised to find that it breaks with intentional analysis and inaugurates a *speculative system* of history (and a fairly mediocre one at that).

III.

We recall how Hegel had already responded to the Husserlian pretention to originarity: Fink's critique already suggests such a response, and the Marxist critique completes it. At issue here, as Thao saw quite clearly, is the problem of *matter. Leben,* as the ground of the meaning of life, is not relieved of its ambiguity and the risk of subjectivism unless it is identified with matter. But phenomenology cannot tolerate such a move, since it represents the abandonment of intentional analysis (of the *ego cogito*) and the passage to speculative metaphysics. In reality, intentional analysis and the "evidence" of the *cogito* are no less elements of speculative philosophy. In the face of this intuitive method and its tenet, dialectical logic asserts its adequation with the real in taking it as an emanation from the real. Phenomenology already had a presentiment of this fact in defining truth as movement, genesis, and recovery; but here again it equivocated—not because this movement is itself equivocal, as phenomenology pretends, but because phenomenology refuses to restore it its material reality. In locating the source of meaning in the interstices between the objective and subjective, it has not realized that the objective (and not the existential) already contains the subjective as negation and as overcoming, and that matter is itself meaning. Far from surpassing them, then, phenomenology is retrograde with respect to Hegelian and Marxist philosophies. This regression is explained historically.

IV.

We emphasized from the outset that the notion of a prepredicative, a prereflective, could be as easily developed against science as for it: this is where the two currents of phenomenology part. This duality is particularly manifest in the way the human sciences are approached. But it is clear that the fruitfulness of phenomenology does not lie on the side of those pursuing the stale, ridiculous arguments of theology and spiritualist philosophy. The value of phenomenology, its "positive side," lies in its effort to recover humanity itself, beneath any objectivist schema, which the human sciences can never recover; and any dialogue with phenomenology clearly must take place on this basis. The interpretive appropriation of data from neuro- and psychopathology, ethnology and sociology, linguistics (which we did not have occasion to discuss here), history, etc.—to the extent that it is neither a crude obscurantism nor an eclecticism without theoretical solidity—meets the demands of a concrete philosophy quite well. And if Merleau-Ponty returns to Marx's famous formula—"We cannot eliminate philosophy without realizing it"[5]—it is because phenomenology seems to signify for him a philosophy *made real,* a philosophy eliminated as a separated existence.[6]

---

5. Maurice Merleau-Ponty, "Marxisme et Philosophie" in *Sens et Non-Sens,* pp. 235 ff.; [English translation: "Marxism and Philosophy" in *Sense and Non-Sense,* pp. 133 ff.].

6. We know that Marx made this doing away with philosophy subsequent to doing away with the specialized thinker, and this in turn was subordinated to the constitution of the classless society.

Bibliography

[Note: Abbreviations employed in the book are listed at the beginning of bibliographic entries.]

Raymond Aron, *[IPH] Introduction à la Philosophie de l'Histoire* (Gallimard, 1938) [English translation: G. J. Irwin, trans., *Introduction to the Philosophy of History* (Beacon Press, 1961)].

Martin Heidegger, *[BT] Sein und Zeit* (Neomarius; 8th ed., 1957 [originally 1927]) [English translation: J. Macquarrie and E. Robinson, trans., *Being and Time* (Harper and Row, 1962)].

Edmund Husserl, *Logische Untersuchungen* (Niemeyer, 1900/1901) [English translation: J. N. Findlay, trans., *Logical Investigations* (Humanities Press, 1970)].

———. *[TC] Zur Phänomenologie des Inneren Zeitbewusstseins* (Niemeyer, 1928) [English translation: J. Churchill, trans., *The Phenomenology of Internal Time Consciousness* (Indiana University Press, 1964)].

———. *[Ideas I] Ideen zu einer reinen Phänomenologie und phänomenologischen Philosophie, I. Buch: Allgemeine Einführung in die reine Phänomenologie* (Niemayer, 1913) [English translation: F. Kersten, trans., *Ideas Pertaining to a Pure Phenomenology and to a Phenomenological Philosophy, First Book: General Introduction to a Pure Phenomenology* (Martinus Nijhoff, 1983)].

———. *Formale und Tranzendentale Logik. Versuch einer Kritik der Logischen Vernunft* (Niemayer, 1979) [English translation: Dorian Cairns, trans., *Formal and Transcendental Logic* (Martinus Nijhoff, 1969)].

———. *[Ideas II] Ideen zu einer reinen Phänomenologie und phänomenologischen Philosophie, II. Buch: Phänomenologische Untersuchungen zur Konstitution* (Martinus Nijhoff, 1952) [English translation: R. Rojcewicz and A. Schuwer, trans., *Ideas Pertaining to a Pure Phenomenology and to a Phenomenological Philosophy,*

Second Book: Studies in the Phenomenology of Constitution (Martinus Nijhoff, 1989)].

———. *Cartesianische Meditationen* (Husserliana, Vol. 1: Matinus Nijhoff, 1950) [English translation: Dorian Cairns, trans., *Cartesian Meditations* (Martinus Nijhoff, 1960)].

———. *[Crisis] Die Krisis der Europäischen Wissenschaft und die tranzendentale Phänomenologie: Eine Einleitung in die phänomenologische Philosophie* (Martinus Nijhoff, 1954) [English translation: D. Carr, trans., *The Crisis of European Sciences and Transcendental Phenomenology: An Introduction to Phenomenological Philosophy* (Northwestern University Press, 1970)].

———. *Erfahrung und Urteil* (Claassen, 1954) [English translation: J. Churchill and K. Ameriks, trans., *Experience and Judgment* (Northwestern University Press, 1973)].

Maurice Merleau-Ponty, *[PP] Phénoménologie de la Perception* (Gallimard, 1945) [English translation: Colin Smith, trans., *Phenomenology of Perception* (Routledge and Kegan Paul, 1962)].

———. *Humanisme et Terreur* (Gallimard, 1947) [English translation: J. O'Neill, trans., *Humanism and Terror* (Beacon Press, 1969)].

———. *Sens et Non-Sens* (Nagel, 1948) [English translation: H. Dreyfus and P. A. Dreyfus, trans., *Sense and Non-Sense* (Northwestern University Press, 1964)].

———. *Les Aventures de la Dialectique* (Gallimard, 1955) [English translation: Joseph Bien, trans., *Adventures of the Dialectic* (Northwestern University Press, 1973)].

———. *Signes* (Gallimard, 1960) [English translation: R. C. McCleary, trans., *Signs* (Nrothwestern University Press, 1964)].

———. *The Primacy of Perception,* J. M. Edie, ed. (Northwestern University Press, 1964).

Jean-Paul Sartre, *La Transcendence de l'Ego* (Vrin, 1965 [originally 1937]) [English translation: F. Williams and R. Kirkpatrick, trans., *The Transcendence of the Ego* (Noonday Press, 1957)].

———. *Esquisse d'une Théorie des Emotions* (Hermann, 1939) [English translation: Philip Mairet, trans., *Sketch for a Theory of the Emotions* (Methuen, 1962)].

———. *L'Imaginaire: Psychologie Phénoménologique de l'Imagination* (Gallimard, 1940) [English translation: Bernard Frechtman, trans.,

The Psychology of Imagination (Philosophical Library, 1948)].

————. *[BN] L'Etre et le Néant* (Gallimard, 1943) [English translation: H. E. Barnes, trans., *Being and Nothingness* (Philosophical Library, 1956)].

Index

Kardner, Abram, 106–109
knowledge, 31, 32, 41, 47
knowledge, scientific, 38
Koffka, Kurt, 83, 86

language, 91
law of essence, 49
Leben, 134, 135
Lebenswelt, 2, 61, 67, 85, 92, 124
Leibniz, Gottfried Wilhelm von, 41
 and Mathesis Universalis, 60
Levinas, Emmanuel, 8, 34
Levi-Strauss, Claude, 105
libido, 92, 93
lifeworld, 2, 61, 123, 124, 127
 see *Lebenswelt,* 57
lived-body, 58
lived-experience, 79, 129
logical empiricists, 92
Lukàcs, Georg, 25 n. 40, 125, 126
Lyotard, Jean-François, 1–19
 Discours, Figure, 7, 12
 Economie libidinal, 7, 12
 Heidegger and the 'jews', 12, 33
 Just Gaming, 12
 Peregrinations, 1, 7, 9
 Pouvoir Ouvrier, 11
 Rudiments paiens, 7
 Socialisme ou Barbarie, 11

Mach, Ernst, 126
Marx, Karl, 18 n. 3, 19 n. 3, 19 n. 4,
 129, 136
Marxism, 4, 10, 17, 20 n. 10, 31, 32, 89,
 119, 123, 125, 127, 133
materialism, 17, 123, 126
mathematical 'objects', 39
mathematics, 38, 40
 pure, 44
Mathesis Universalis, 6, 32, 41, 43, 60
matrix of intersubjectivity, 19 n. 4
matter, 135
Mauss, Marcel, 105, 106, 109
 The Gift, 105
meaning, 10, 65, 87, 90, 93, 98, 99,
 120, 123, 124, 125

ambiguous, 121
 assumption of, 98
 in process, 116
mediation, 66, 91
memory, 114
Merleau-Ponty, Maurice, 2, 4, 8, 10,
 12, 13, 19 n. 4, 20 n. 7, 20 n. 8, 21 n.
 10, 22 n. 20, 22 n. 21, 23 n. 28, 23 n.
 29, 23 n.24, 24 n. 30, 31, 32, 33, 68,
 69, 78, 80, 83–86, 91, 98, 101–103,
 114, 124, 128, 129, 131, 136
 Humanism and Terror, 4, 129
 Phenomenology of Perception, 4,
 10, 13, 90, 93, 106, 114, 129
 The Structure of Behavior, 89
method, 5, 90, 96, 97, 98, 100
 empiricist, 95
methods, objective experimental, 34
middle, 13, 14
Mill, John Stuart, 74, 95
Mitsein, 103, 104, 106, 117, 120, 130,
 134
Müller-Lyer phenomenon, 82
mundane, 2, 41, 42, 45, 47, 49, 53, 80

narratives, 5
natural attitude, 45–47, 54
natural object, 47
natural thesis, 46
natural world, 63
necessity, 49
Neo-Kantians, 44, 52
noema, 55, 80, 113
noesis, 55, 80, 113

object, 39, 44, 48, 49, 89, 112
 immanence of, 65
 unity of the thing, 58
objectivism, 78, 99, 133
objectivity, 31, 32, 56, 131
object-pole, 55
ontology, 41, 100
originary givenness, 40
originary social, 100–104
 as ground of all social scientific
 knowledge, 100–101

Other, 57–59, 75, 76, 89, 100–103, 130
  otherness of, 57

Pavlov, Ivan Petrovich, 81
perception, 39, 45, 48, 85, 86
  unity of, 90
personality
  as integrated totality, 108
  see I, cogito, self, 108
perspectives
  flux of, cf. *Abschattungen,* 8, 16,
    47, 51
phenomena, 32, 91
phenomenological attitude, 51
phenomenological reflection, 52, 79
phenomenology, 2, 4, 5, 6, 10, 17, 32,
    43, 65, 74, 75, 76, 80, 83, 100, 113,
    122, 135
  accents of, 8, 34
  ambiguities of, 33, 92
  and attempts to overcome individ-
    ual-society antinomy, 106
  and history, 111–132
  and Marxism, 123–132
  and physiology, 89–92
  and psychoanalysis, 92–94
  and psychology, 77–94
  and sociology, 95–109
  and the double Cartesian heritage,
    60
  and the opposition of reflection
    and introspection, 79
  as a logic, 74
  as eidetic science, 76
  as logical introduction to human
    sciences, 76
  as philosophy of ambiguity, 127
  as philosophy of cogito, 75
  as reprise for experimentation, 76
  as science of consciousness, 65–69
  definition of, 32
  historical significance of, 8
  imposes its own ambiguity on his-
    tory, 133
  phenomenology of, 7
  posing ambiguous history, 133

positive side of, 2, 136
situated in history, 123
truths of, 16
two faces of, 33, 135
unity of, 33
philosophy, 60, 76
  and sociology, 104
  as worldview, 73
  eliminated as a separate existence,
    18, 136
  of history, 119
physicalism, 86
physics, 40, 41, 44, 60
Piaget, Jean, 103
Platonism, 37, 41, 42
pleasure principle, 93
positivism, 73, 126
postmodern condition, 5, 18
poststructuralism, 5
pragmatism, 31, 73, 126
pragmatist-empiricist prejudice, 40
prehistory, 84
prejudices, 60
prepredicative, 33, 135
prereflective, 33, 135
present, 116
principle of immanence, 53
profiles, 8, 16, 47, 48
psychoanalysis, 17, 20 n. 10
  Freudian, 92
psychologism, 31, 37, 40, 43, 44, 73, 86
psychologistic subjectivism, 51
psychology, 52, 75, 79, 88, 106
  gestalt, 81–87
pure eidetic form, 41
pure logic, 41
putting in parentheses, 6, 31, 47, 51

radical beginnings, 3, 132
radicalism, 46
radical reflections, 2, 18, n. 3
real, 55, 83
realism, 37, 44
reality, 125
  ambiguity of, 124
  hidden, 67